AF199857

Marianne E. Meyer
Beyond Death
How my husband showed me from beyond
that life continues after death

Production and Publishing
BoD - Books on Demand, Norderstedt
ISBN 978-3-744840798

Author and publisher do not accept any liability for damages of any kind which arise directly or indirectly from the application or use of the information in this work.

Some other books by M. E. Meyer:

Family Code – Death is Not the End

How Water Connects our Worlds

Migrant Birds on Wheels

Cranberry Power Fruit

Spirulina, Überlebensnahrung für ein neues Zeitalter

So verbindet Wasser unsere Welten

Psyllium - So bekommen Sie Ihr Fett weg

Wunderwesen Wasser: Clusterwasser stoppt Allergie, Alzheimer, Krebs...

Marianne E. Meyer, Apartado 320, P-8801 Tavira

Marianne Erika Meyer studied pedagogy in Frankfurt when she got to know and love her husband when buying a car. In the mid-1980s they moved to California for ten years. There, the author studied nutritional science. Her doctoral thesis on immune defense and Spirulina she published in her bestseller *Spirulina, das blaugrüne Wunder.* She lived alternately in southern Hesse, Morocco and in a farmhouse in Portugal working at times with behavioral adolescents. Now next to writing Marianne cares for wild cats and dogs. The sudden transition of her beloved husband into the spiritual world and his after-death communication directed her focus to spirituality.

Picture Credits
Cover: C.-P. Meyer, E. F. Braun
R. Taylor S. 3, E. F. Braun S. 21,24,43,62,63, B. Dodge S. 25, K. Sten 55
NASA 73
Layout and Typography: M. Meyer

Marianne E. Meyer
BEYOND DEATH

How my husband showed me from the
beyond that life continues after death

TABLE OF CONTENTS

Prologue

For each one of us at some point, the decisive question arises, whether or in what form we will live on after this life. Since in our maternal family most of us are psychics I've always been interested in the connection between life on earth and beyond, especially in the question of the meaning and purpose of our existence on earth. For my extrasensory experiences, I searched and found numerous confirmation in the relevant literature. Therefore I'm convinced death is not the end but a transitional stage to living on the other side. A few months after my father had left his body, my mother reported on her after-death contact (ADC):

"Just before waking up I saw a hedge. I looked through it, swirled upwards in a pull and landed on a green meadow. Everything was as on earth only the colors were more intense. I walked along a path and suddenly there stood our old kitchen cabinet. Ludi was sitting on the recess in the middle. He said I wait for you until you are ready."

I had a similar situation with my late husband, but about that, I'll tell you a little later. Now I'd like to give the doubters a ray of hope and consolation. For, if they someday go on their way to the after-world, it will help them to find their bearings.

In January 1987, the National Opinion Research Center conducted a survey prepared by Andrew Greeley. This survey of the Catholic priest, well-known in the USA, was published in the February issue of the American Health magazine. According to the results, 42% of adult Americans believe they once before have had contact with a deceased. The respondents to the study of Judy and Bill Guggenheim impressively described the memorable events of their so-called after-death communication which the authors shared in the book "Hello from Heaven: A New Field of Research - After-Death Communication Confirms That Life and Love Are Eternal" in twelve main forms. They distinguish contacts with present feeling, hearing, touching and smelling perceptions, visual contacts of different design, visions, after-death contacts in half-sleep and sleep, out-of-body and telephone exchange and finally symbolic contacts and physical phenomena mostly associated with electricity. I would be delighted if my after-death contacts and those of my relatives and friends, especially those with a strength of evidence, can take away the fear of dying and comfort you. The after-death contacts of my family members are of different nature. My grandnephews Moritz and Jonas had contact with deceased relatives in their preschool years. My cousin Karin saw her Hans-Hermann leaning happily on a tree at his funeral. He appeared as a poltergeist for a year, also when Karin had guests. My mother had one of her last after-death contacts with my father, who materialized in the bathroom when she was sitting in the bathtub. He was naked and white from head to toe. I have ghost experiences often on the PC, probably because I spend most of the time on the computer and when writing I'm most relaxed. Like my mother, thirty years before (see page 11), I also had after-death contacts without knowledge of the death message, as described in my book on the family code on page 101 ff.

On November 11, just before 11 a. m., I went to the fitness room of our residential complex. The 911 girl was on the treadmill. I said: "Did you have last night's service?" She replied: "Oh my God, what a Wednesday! I did not have a quiet minute. It was not even my shift. I covered for a colleague." I asked: "Can't you sleep now?" She said:"No, I still have a job at a restaurant in Redondo Beach. I am in a hurry. Can you return the key, please?" "Sure." A moment later I became restless and was no longer in the mood for the machines. I dropped the key into Sandi's mailbox. In front of our apartment door, I met Peter. Are you leaving? No, I just want to repair my Firebird. *Inside, the wall clock from Jerry's garage showed 11:10 a. m. Together with a toaster, popcorn machine, pans, bowls, and plates, it found a more meaningful existence with us.*

On my way to the bathroom, I passed by our brand new queen-size bed. Out of the blue, I dead stalled! I couldn't move my extremities and collapsed onto the bed. My body felt like filled up with liquid led. The faint fear of being seriously ill only lasted a second. Following a hunch, I addressed the thin air: Lisa is that you? The eerie episode ended on the spot. Arms and legs were lax again. Was it providence that I'd just read Ambrose Worrall's book? He was a clairvoyant working as a mechanical engineer. One of his co-workers on his way home for lunch was hit by a train without realizing his being dead. Coming back to work, he was upset since his colleagues did not respond. Ambrose saw him grabbing through the tools and did send him back to the railway crossing. So he could see what had happened to him. Through this I learned, when we someday irrevocably leave our material body, it can happen that we do not consciously notice our being out-of-body. As in sudden death when involved in an accident, having a heart attack, or being intoxicated by alcohol or drugs. Such deceased are confused because they want to go on with their habits but are not noticed by their relatives, friends or colleagues. Thus leading to spook. (Family Code, p. 90)

I felt odd talking to my mother-in-law's spirit: You've left your bedridden body. You can now travel as fast as you think. As the minutes passed, I wasn't as sure anymore. Was that for real? An hour later the phone rang. Jochen confirmed Lisa's passing. I said it was about an hour ago. Jochen said I don't know. They just

9

called from the hospital. It was 11 minutes past 11 our time when I felt your mother's transition. I called my mother and told her about Lisa's haunting. Isn't it amazing she'd chosen this date? Uh-huh! She knew that Peter has a hard time memorizing dates. He surely won't forget the beginning of carnival. I was paralyzed but only for a sec.

Ma said: When Mamme passed on I had that too. I know. But I was 20 minutes immobile like glued to a chair. My colleagues in the textile factory did not know what to do. (ibidem)

Recently walking the dogs another after-death contact crossed my mind. It was on November 11, 2007. I worked on the PC on my book "Water Code Cracked?" Suddenly two photos turned into XX. Shortly after I realized that it was Lisa's 20th day of death: twice X Roman 10 makes 20. Immediately, I lit a white candle as I mostly do on death-days of friends and relatives. Lately, my late husband has comforted me with even more conclusive interactions.

Initial shock and first encounter

On February 11, 2017, we were in the middle of the preparation of our Morocco tour. The camper was packed, scooter, and bike stowed in the rear garage. Peter wanted to recharge the battery. Since it had rained for a long time, some water had once again entered the bedroom. I was about to wipe the floor when I noticed Peter's exclamation and the sound of his falling in front of the entry door. I thought he had slipped on the wet tiles. I tried to help him up. When I asked him what had happened, he did not answer; saliva bubbled from his mouth. I immediately called Peter's brother, who came with his wife a little later. We carried out attempts at resuscitation. But when I supplied my beloved husband with my breath, it was already clear to me that there was no longer any

10

hope of continuing our nearly 44-year life together. The men of the emergency ambulance could not do anything either. When they took him to the ambulance, his brother cried supported by his daughter. I was just looking at them in shock. All my senses were on strike.

In the morgue of the hospital in Faro, Peter laid there as peacefully sleeping with a smile on his lips. After I had said goodbye with a last kiss, the thought came to me that everything should be like this and that everything is good and Peter will still help and support me. It was only later that I thought it was a thought transfer. For years, we had the experience that one of us expressed something that the other thought.

In an e-mail, Carole wrote I should hold one hand on the heart and one on the solar plexus, looking in the northern direction and call for Peter.

In the early morning of Feb 17, Peter showed me his light-flooded new environment in his faded white-gray bad boy T-shirt and the Bermudas he had worn in California. In the book *Hello from Heaven: A New Field of Research-After-Death Communication Confirms That Life and Love Are Eternal* I became aware that the deceased often wear the clothes which are of importance to the people to whom they appear. The surrounding Peter walked with me uphill reminded me of the dunes of Erg Chebbi in Morocco. Peter loved the desert almost as much as the sea. He was always happy finding desert flowers.

These clothes are very special to me. In this outfit, my bad-boy hubby compensated his nicotine withdrawal with vodka and was almost shot in a balmy Californian summer night almost. As a result of this incisive experience, we almost separated, as can be seen on the water crystal photo on page 26.

Everything around us breathed in brightness and light. Peter beamed at me in a happy mood and said: "It's always nice and warm here." I would have liked to stay with him.

This experience lessened the pain of my grave loss a little making the grief more tolerable. But not the despair, the fact that I miss Peter so much. I don't need to worry about him anymore, no more driving too fast or swimming too far out. I just have to cope with my grief and get my life back on track. I'm torn between the hope the book may help me and the fear it moves me too much. But since the telepathic transfer in the morgue, I think Peter wants that too. After all, I hope not only to help me but also to all the other bereaved. For as long as a relationship may last, at any time, the day comes when one has to go. And then it is a consolation to know that our loved ones are nearby for a while and still part of life or waiting for us.

In the morning I turned on the light and read a few lines in Eliot Pattison's book "The Foreign Tibetan" when the light on the nightstand went off suddenly. I put the glasses away and put me aside. I said, "Do we want to spoon or what is it?" When the little owl howled, I said: "Oh Jacob" and Bob's your uncle, the light was on again. It has not been so long since Peter began to call the little owl Jacob. I said, "What makes you think that?" He said, "Karl always says that."

Did Peter realize about his end and considered this as a possibility to contact me. I'd always told him that my mother wanted to make me aware of something with the light. Of course, I now take much more attention to any signs.

In the evening I had a talk show running, but wrote e-mails and did not look at all. Peter did not like talk shows. For work on the

PC that is little intellectually demanding, talk shows are ideal, because I do not have to look. Suddenly there was a sound as if something light fell over. About a minute later the TV went off. If I had looked up at the noise, I would have noticed the automatic switch off sign on the TV. A little later I saw what the sound was. The mourning card with Peter's photo leaning diagonally against the urn was tilted forward. But that it should have fallen by itself is technically not possible, because I had closed all windows and doors and there was no draft.

On Saturday, February 18, a week later, the time before and around Peter's last hour was difficult to bear. I was totally tied up in knots and dazed. Fortunately, an e-mail came from a singing mate, who opened the floodgates again. Our choir has about fifty members. So, thankfully, I received a large number of heartwarming devotions, and I now know that it is very comforting for the bereaved to be not alone at certain times or have telephone or e-mail contacts. Peter was always a welcome groupie for the choir. He sometimes filmed us at our shows and shot the photos for our flyers. He's driven me to the choir rehearsal in the Café Zé in Luz de Tavira. In the meanwhile, he read the German newspaper in the library, did some grocery shopping, came back for me, drank a glass of red wine for 50 cents, and chatted with the choir members.

Today it is strange that apart from the e-mails the internet is not working meaning I can not work on any book where I need translation or grammar support. At the moment, there is only the grief book. But is such a thing possible? So far, it has always been that the internet is either working or not at all. Also, the Google boys and girls could not help me on this question. Renate, who had visited me, was also surprised at this phenomenon because that had

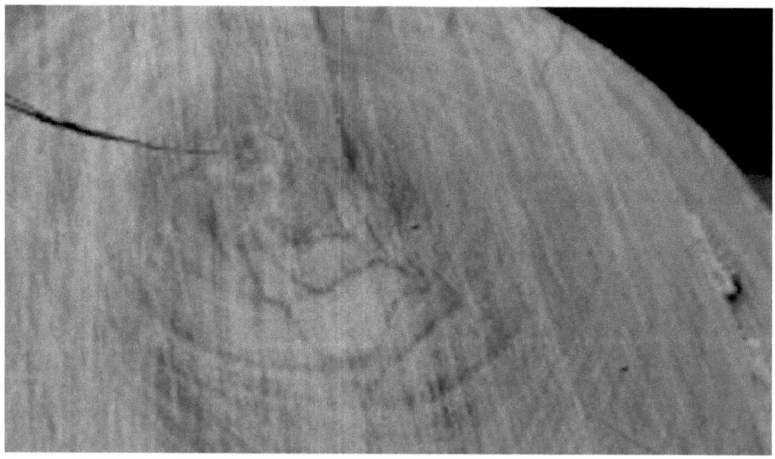

14

never happened to her as well. Then the thing with the saw: I saw a thick branch in the morning.

After a long pause, I finished the work at about 1:30 p. m. In both saw surfaces, I recognized a sign I had discovered in water crystal photos pointing to the death of a person or an animal: a dark circle with a light dot in the center. The tunnel with the light. Unfortunately, the third photo with the better piece, where the dark ring was more clearly visible, was still on the new smartphone. But that was broken when I wanted to recharge it since the power plant by accident installed a power line. It also shows the beginning when painting a rose. I immediately remembered Peter's course with his uncle, the painter Adolf Meyer from Gauting, to whom he owes one of his many first names. He had shown his nephew how easy it is to paint a rose. Also strange: parts of the same branch made such different pictures. These may not be evidence of an after-death contact. But on the 11th day, after his transition to the spiritual world Peter made me happy with his undeniable significance:

After-death contacts with significance

In the morning of February 22, Isabel Bannier-Groß, the daughter of Peter Groß who won the gold medal at the inventor's fair in Geneva in 2007, called. She and her husband had visited us in the previous winter of 2016. Isa had just checked her e-mails and got to know the sad news. When she asked m how I was doing, I cried asking: "Why should I stay here?"

Isa recommended certain pills that had helped her with the loss of her son, Christian. Suddenly she said excited, "Mary, I just see Peter." "Huh?" "He looks quite happy, laughing as always. He has his red wine glass in his hand and points to a hut which he shares with another man. But he wants to find something for himself. Peter has a bright t-shirt with a little gray, looks like stains." "What? I saw him like that on the 6th day. I walked with him, everything was bright and warm, but I knew I had only visited him on the other side." Isa said," That is strange, Peter shows me you painting something. You wear dark leggings and a long-sleeved sweater. I see the colors blue and yellow. "

At first, I did not know what Isa meant. When she called for a second time saying she had sent the pills, it had occurred to me in the meantime. I had friends here for coffee and cake. Rineke and Wendy from our Shanty choir wanted to see me and offered their help. Since the cistern had some ugly stains from rainwater and snails, I whitened them. The tiles on the edge of the cistern are indeed blue and yellow! And for painting, I always wear these clothes because they already have stains. I only had them put on for about 20 minutes!

This after-death contact has an enormous significance, as Isabel did not know I was painting. She could not have known if Peter had not told her.

I also asked Peter questions. How he wants to have his obituary. Isa said: "He wants not so much in detail, childhood only very briefly, he would like you to write a biography of the dealership in Frankfurt and Los Angeles later on." I said, "I do not know the details at all." Isa said, "he shows me a TV show with cars. If these broadcasts are late at night and you're not too tired, you should always have pen and paper at hand. When snow appears on-screen, write down the gray letters."

I said: "I've seen something like this, just a few weeks ago with Peter. I said to Peter the letters could be ghost messages. Perhaps Bolko wants to tell us something. He did not say anything then. Usually, he said, you and your esoteric babble."

Isa said, "there's a Mediterranean-looking man with Peter, he has pepper and salt hair." I said, "this can be Bolko. He'd been born with Peter in the same delivery room 20 minutes before him and collapsed walking dog five years ago."

After 15 to 20 minutes of conversation, Isa said: Peter signals that he must leave now for a kind of training. He seems to have little desire to do so. I see it on his face. He also throws his hand over his shoulder. I said, "yes this is his typical sign to say I don't need that. He let me know that it can't be helped it's required. I said, "but please, tell me first how you want the sea burial." Isa said, "Peter wants you to throw the urn openly into the water. He shows me a cancer. He wants the marine animals to settle there. Peter wants a fun celebration. He shows me a wind quartet in black suits and pulls down the corners of his mouth. He doesn't want anything sad." I said: "Yes, he loves the sound of the Rolling Stones, Beach Boys, Dire Straits, and Fleetwood Mac. Since both sons are managers of big companies and have to cope with a heavy workload for the next 8-10 weeks, I think we'll do it between June 9 and 12."

17

I'm just reading a book containing a proven after-death contact of a celebrity. The English writer and journalist W.T. Stead wanted to take part in the Titanic's record ride to write a factual report about it. But he did not come to this because he was among the 1517 victims of that fatal night on the 15th of April. His daughter Estelle has the rare ability to write automatically, by switching off her consciousness. She had already received a message from her father from the beyond in the night following the catastrophe. Over the following weeks, she received more details. Instead of the planned report on the expected record, William Thomas Stead described life after physical life. Estelle added these after-death contacts of her deceased father together in the book The Blue Island: Experiences of a New Arrival Beyond the Veil, so that the writer and journalist posthumously published his experiences, albeit differently than planned. On page 9 of this book is a report about the world famous writer Edgar Wallace. Shortly before his death, he is said to have promised to his friends to make his presence felt from the beyond. He was firmly convinced death is only a transitional stage to the continuation of life in another world. In fact, shortly after his transition, he was supposed to have fulfilled his promise and to have contacted his friends. Unfortunately, Estelle Stead did not mention a source, and the dear friends are, of course, already long in the hereafter. Even on the Internet, I couldn't find anything about after-death contacts of the British writer whose criminal stories were filmed in the 1960s, and in my youth topics of discussions on the schoolyards.

Renée Stellwag, the daughter of my friend Ursula Keim, had a post-death experience at the age of 12. She did not know anyone had died. She thought of some ghost. Because, suddenly the box of bird fodder which always stood in the same place flew out of the shelf in a high arc and fell on the ground, rattling. Renée screamed. Uschi hurried to her room. "What's up?" Renée said: "There must be something wrong. A ghost has thrown the box." An hour later the phone rang. Uschi learned that her stepbrother had died. By the way, until about her mid 20th, Uschi felt earthquakes thousands of miles distant. I once saw her grabbing the rail of her bed, looking odd and asking, didn't you feel that? A few hours later, was reported in the news about another quake. Renée's husband went into the light three years ago. She also had several after-death contacts just like her mother whose husband died two years ago. I had visited both in July and will write about their experiences in another book. If you, dear reader, want to publish your communication with your loved ones in the next book, please let me know, preferably by e-mail:

drmarianneemeyer @ gmail.com

Daniela, a Swiss fellow student, also reported on after-death contacts of relatives even before she's learned of their death. *When someone dies from my family, a crystal glass breaks in my showcase without touching it.* (Family Code, page 13)

On Feb 27, I wondered why the youngest and last still living 90-year-old sister of my mother had not offered her condolences to me. However, I know from my mother that her sisters seldom contacted her. She often said, "if I would not call from time to time or drive to Eberbach, I'd not know having sisters at all." Cousin Heide, the animal communicator who like my mother looks like Doris Day is also as communicative as my mother was and Doris still is. They usually report by phone, e-mails or letters. Since Peter's transition, cousin Karin has often communicated with me via Facebook. Twenty years ago, after her Hans-Hermann had shot himself after the Chernobyl clearing work, she'd experienced a still bigger shock and can help me through her compassion through the hardest time.

19

2-28, 11.10: I forced myself to have breakfast because I've got to eat something. I do not smell anything yet nor can I taste any-thing, but the body needs some food. The phone comes to life. Isa asks, "Mary, how are you?" I murmur: "Carry on forever, Isa." Excited Isa exclaimed, "I have to tell you something. I'm just sit-ting on the PC and suddenly have a book cover in front of my eyes. It looks like black and white, but it's brownish. "I throw in: "Do you mean old photos, sepia? "Isa replies," Yeah, right. There is SAD NEWS written in large white letters. Below: water crys-tal, but I see it slanting. I do not know how it goes on. Beneath Dr. Marianne Meyer. I murmur: "But I do not use the doctoral de-gree on my books." Isa ignores it: "I see Peter's face, but it's nei-ther painted nor a photo. More like a computer drawing from the police. I say, "Could it be one of Ernst Braun's water crystal pho-tos? I already have one in profile when Peter had a ponytail. I've shown it in the book Wasser-Code geknackt? At that time I sent only my signature on a note to the art studio in Switzerland. Ernst Braun placed neutral water in a vial on it. After a day, with a pipette, he dripped 22 drops in 22 Petri dishes, put them in a freezer for 3-4 hours then took pics under a microscope. He ob-tained 15 photos. They showed my sun sign, markers of my life, preferences and character traits. The one with Peter in profile shows a hard time in our life. The water crystal photo resembles Emoto's one, obtained by H2O, which had been provided with the sound of the Elvis Song Heartbreak Hotel. I recognized ob-jects reminding me of an uneasy period in life with Peter in Cali-fornia during which he had been smoking and compensated the nicotine withdrawal with alcohol.

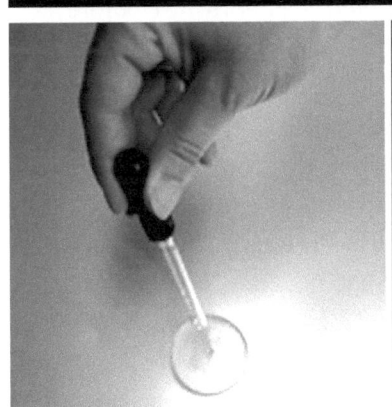

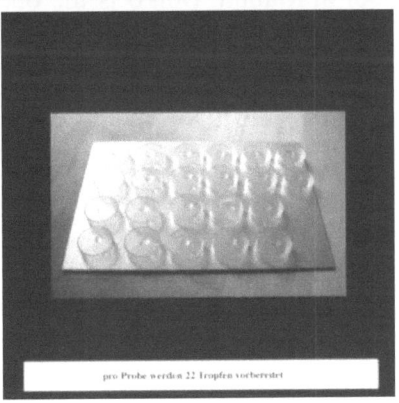

pro Probe werden 22 Tropfen vorbereitet

21

The cut-out of the broken crystal represents Peter's shadow image. At that time we had almost separated. "No," Isa replies, "I see him from the front." I said: "With a cap?"

"No, it's like a phantom picture. The font on the back is also white. It is DIN A 5 and a solid cover, about one and a half inch thick. "Hardcover?" "Yes, if they say so. It does not look like your other ones. The guy I met with Peter is here. He shows you at a table with the books and a lot of people, could be at the book fair. You write a lot of personal things in the books."

"Yes, he's nodding." I said: "Yes, he's been there for five years. I once read that we rejuvenate in the hereafter. I think it was in Stead's book, the well-known editor, who had perished with the Titanic."

"Well, Mary, he makes the money sign." I said: "Yes, Bolko and Peter could not handle money. Bolko had given away lots of gifts like expensive watches, leather clothes and wasted money in restaurants without any prospect of success. I am only thinking of Bollos Pollos, the interior of the finest quality, but Bolko probably wolfed down most of the chickens. And all of the money Peter had lent and invested in funky companies would be a luxury villa with pool in Malibu. Bolko is the one who was born just before Peter and had collapsed at the age of 70. " Isa said, "yes, he nods. Does he have anything to do with Peter about money?"

Perhaps the matter with Ubbe, where Bolko as a lawyer had lost the case and now the honorarium from my books is still seized. A former friend bought a car with my eBay address, and I had to take it back, even though we were in Portugal. I had never signed a contract with a Mr. Dressler and had never seen the car. They already have ripped off 3000 or 4000 Euros. I think the car only cost €5000. At the time of the transaction, we were in Portugal and had therefore neither concluded a contract with any buyer nor collected any money. The first judge had decided in my favor, but the tricky opponent won at the higher court. The lawyers Lieb & Koll realized that the guilty one had already done all the oaths, and there was absolutely nothing to be fetched. I understand our friends' daughter Tina. She said, when she was still studying law, I could never be a lawyer, possibly a prosecutor. And she is right. I could not throw a person into misfortune, which I know very well she or he is innocent. My comfort in all worldly injustice is the existence of a supreme judgment: the cosmic law. (Family Code, page 4) I may contact the attorney and report the lawyers since what they did may be fraud. They did send €111 back to the Windpferd Publishing house saying they have received more than I owe. But that must have been a lie or they unjustly still charge the fee of my two Shaker Publishing books which is only about €200-250 per year. Maybe they just want to cash in on the 4% interest. Since I am not aware of any guilt, and I can not do anything for the wrong jurisdiction, I will just tell all my readers and leave it to the cosmic law, what happens next.

Speaking of injustice: In Germany, one of the richest countries in the world, millions of citizens are afraid of their future. Above all, to live in poverty at the end of their long years of work. Many can only dream of a relaxed, happy evening of life.

Neighboring countries grant their retirees a pension that will allow them a dignified, carefree aging. Why is the export world champion not willing to do so? In many neighboring countries, pension payments consist of a basic annuity for everybody and an income-dependent amount. Why can't Germans have it? In a fairness experiment, monkeys respond defiantly, when treated unjustly. Especially chimpanzees are for fair trading transactions even if they get the preference and the other doesn't get equal pay for equal work.

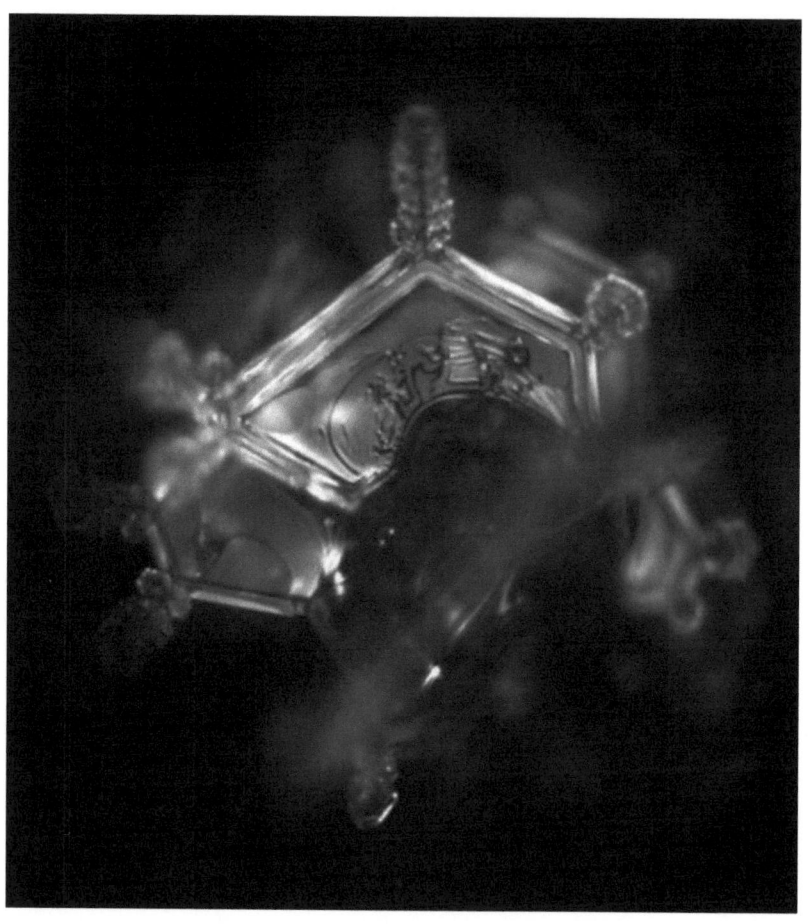

https://www.youtube.com/watch?v=xot4z1CKFMo

If Europe should work such injustice must not exist and should be clear even to politicians.

Sooner rather than later we'll need a global unconditional basic income adapted to economic conditions to counteract the desolate life of many young people without any perspective and their increasing excessive acts of violence.

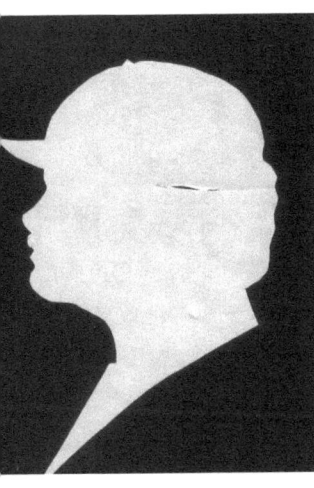

It's a pity that Peter had hidden his round bald head under the baseball cap. The cut-out original fits exactly into the demolition outline.

I can not find a profile photo of Peter showing his left side. But on the Hawaii photo below you can see the indentation on the chin.

Messages via physical phenomena

Dear Anneliese,

Now I know how it is to lose the love of my life. It is harder than I thought, and the whole thing is still very unreal for me. It will take a while to handle that. Peter collapsed on February 11, exactly one week after his 75th birthday in front of our doorstep. On Feb 14, we wanted to go to Morocco. The motorhome was packed. It is quite terrible, after nearly 44 years, to see the dearest person no longer in the usual form. Though Peter's little signs always cheer me up. Yesterday, for instance, I heard a very delicate ringing. Because, I didn't react, after a few seconds again an ethereal jingle. Following an inspiration I looked up the current TV program: God and the world - Theme: The new retirees; active life in old age, the own finitude as a drive, what I still want to reach. Yes, it was a reassuring report. In our family, we obviously need to learn about the loss of our partners. Or do you know anyone in our family where the partner not first died? We must accept our fate. I come to Germany in summer.

Until then, all the best! Have a nice time!

Warmly,

Marianne

3-2: The hammer in the morning when waking up strikes not as strong as before. But also the small things, like e. g. just the advertising for the delivery hero, hits hard. When Peter had finished breakfast in the morning, he called *tatütata, der Lieferheld ist da* or something like that. Even this I don't know if I remember right. I would need massive spiritual help. I'm still having a cold. My

26

bronchial whistle, consistent diarrhea indicates deacidification. I don't know anything about Lisbela, the landlady. When she dies, the son-in-law might sell the house. I've little desire to move. F it's affordable I might even buy it.

3-6 ca. 7.30 p. m.: In the computer a sudden double-tone. "Peter is that you?" Again this delicate double-tone. I immediately googled TV Now. The film *Was Bleibt* (what remains) on Arte leaped to my eye. And as a first picture: a chic living room with a Miller Chair! "Oh, you mean that! And also in black. It would have matched perfectly with our sofas. " As I read later, the film was also about the topic of getting drunk. "Well, Peter this fits perfectly. You have drunk two bottles of red wine almost every evening.

   Maybe the vein in your temple had burst. I do not know anything yet. In Portugal, everything takes a long time. I recently called the hospital. The autopsy results were not there yet. Again the double-tone. I further scrolled down. At DMAX Goldtimer-Wertanlage mit PS, they showed a Mustang, Peter's first car he owned in Hermosa Beach! I didn't have to wait a minute for both stations. Miller Chair and Mustang were immediately visible. "Right, you said to Isa, that you want to work with me, not only via TV but also via PC. You must have already known before, what comes on TV. You seem to have received proper training. Maybe you can do these things so soon because you listened to my psychic experiences all the time. Even if you did not believe it, you were not quite as surprised as others, who cannot find their way at first. And Bolko has probably informed you too."

   "At first, I thought you had once again contacted me because of my bad patch since I'd cleared the dying clothes and carried some shoes into the camper to make room for me to sleep in the dressing room because I had to clean the bedroom for Ines. Can it be that you have foreseen my mood already? At least I thank you!"

27

3-7: For the first time, I felt a sparkle of happiness when I woke up, though the serotonin production of my neurons was extremely marginal. If I get a message from Peter every few days, I'll probably get through the whole thing sane. Yesterday, when I'd put the giant lemon in the fruit bowl, I remembered I'd dreamed about it before. I had taken it from the tree by mistake. I just wanted to touch it, but the heavy fruit fell off. I must have suppressed the circumstances quickly. When I dreamed of Maritas and Theo's accidents, I had seen it quite clearly and told some people.

I still have no sense of smell and taste.

Relief by consolation

I was pleased with the e-mails from friends of the choir as I was able to cry again and again. So I already detoxicated. Therefore I may be better off with Barbara Simonsohn's offer for the Reiki seminar Freebie instead of the deacidification seminar since emotional tears contain a lot of poison.

Hello Marianne,

How are you? Surely you've settled the things that were spontaneous to settle. I hope the funeral was dignified. Now comes the routine of everyday life, the gap is there, and you are slowly becoming aware of how much Peter is missing. Hopefully, you have support and faithful accompaniment, someone you can go to, just so without having to speak. Sure you still think sometimes, he comes right away. It takes a long time to realize that it is a definitive leaving. Then comes the long process of farewell and the new construction of your life. You must live through all phases. Much weeping and saying goodbye. You can only do this by yourself. I wish you a lot of strength.

Greetings from here, Gabi

Dear Gabi,

Many thanks for your support. You are very kind. In a few hours, it will be four weeks. The sea burial will take some time. Peter's sons want to come together. They are managers of big companies and occupied for the next eight to ten weeks. So I guess we'll do it in June. In the last three days, I've had Ines, my wealthy er-satz-daughter from California here. She and her hubby own 2000charge, a company similar to PayPal. She gave me pleasure when shopping, even for the animals. The money for the castra-tion of our new family member Tobi she has also left.

My landlady Lisbela who lived 400 m away from me moved to her daughter to the 7 km distant Tavira. The dog, she had kept on the thick iron chain for years, they just let loose. Naturally, he trotted in my direction, for whenever I came, I often brought a treat and promised him if Lisbela is no longer there to take him. He is about five years old and always wants to mount Mia. That is why I have an appointment with the veterinarian on Friday. I won-der why Tobi acts normal after all the years on the chain. Peter contacts me from time to time. That helps of course. When I had Ines from California and Helga from Hanover visiting, he did not get in touch.

Yours deeply, Marianne

3-11: Four weeks and still my sense of smell and taste has not re-turned. However, I've noticed a very slight scent of freesia, when I had stuck my nose right into the blooms. Last year I could smell the flowers from the front door ten yards away.

Dear Hedi,

The worst I have behind me, even though my smell has still not returned. The taste has been slightly better since yesterday. The markets and restaurants where we always came together, I was frightened to think about, but it was nice today. I sat next to Karl and asked him if he'd be next, he should try hard so he could help Loni the way Peter is helping me: "Go to Loni, look at what she is doing. If it's something out of the ordinary, show it to me. So I can tell her." In his Bavarian slang, Karl said," Moanst du dös kriag i hi? (Do you think I can do it?"). I answered," Peter did it, and he did not quite believe in an afterlife.

I didn't say anything, but Karl looked blindingly merry. He is going to celebrate his birthday on the 16th and invited me and Sigrid, who is also alone and now doing things with me. I did not say anything because I told them when visiting me in the first week that I've experienced this with Peter for the 4th time that people look notably good shortly before their transition. I hope today it was only a biorhythms high and Karl will be alive for a long time. If Peter cannot drink the champagne any- more at least Karl should enjoy it.

Warm regards, also to Rudi

Marianne

Rudi had made another bet. Once, Hedi's hubby had already lost a bottle of champagne because he bet silver would go up to €50. This time he bet that the Commerzbank will be broke within two years. I remember it well since Peter said: "I don't think I'll live that long. The certainty in his voice shocked me, and I reacted harshly. Maybe that's why Peter didn't tell me about his forthcoming leaving. Since at Christmas 2017, the two years are over, and Rudi and Hedi will visit the champagne will probably flow again.

For over a month I wondered why Jerry did not reply to my e-mail. Then I got one from his daughter Linda: *I am terribly sorry for your loss. I knew Peter from trips we all took together, and I often thought he was very lucky to find you – his soul mate.*

When my dad passed away on March 7th, my world had changed forever. I have never experienced such sadness, and I am sure you have not either. Perhaps we can comfort each other by thinking now my dad and Peter are together in the afterlife. Both telling each other funny stories.

In another e-mail, Linda told me something about her bitch Penny. She loved Jerry very much not only because he brought her treats once a week. Four hours before he died, she was in Jerry's favorite chair at her last gasp. He must have been pleased to be greeted by Penny and Peter in his new environment.

Setbacks and the usual chaos of grief

On March 13 at 16:30 I thought the worst would be over. But when watering the trees Peter had planted, I was realizing the finitude and broke into a passion of tears. Almost as bad as a week ago when Renate came and I couldn't find the completed form for the application for the pension which I had forgotten in a folder.

3-15: Yesterday's singing with the seniors and the children was quite emotional mainly because so many singing friends had hugged and kissed me feeling so sorry for me. As in the rehearsal, I could not sing the last verse of The Rose of Tralee. Since it was such a difficult day with many tears, I took ½ of Isa's pills in the evening.

Just now I was reading my blog report borreliosis article in which my mother plays an important role. Suddenly again a double ring, but a higher and clearer sound louder. Huh? I immediately googled TV Jetzt. It was 9:00 clock sharp. I switched on the TV, and what beamed at me at first in the ARD channel? *STURM DER LIEBE*, the soap opera my mother always

31

watched when my father had made his transition to the spiritual world. Okay, why not borrowing a life for a while, when the own life seems not worth living. So Mom can also ring the bell. And according to her bell-like soprano in a higher tone. Then I watch this telenovela when I do translations or proofreadings. I do not have to think as much and often run the TV. From childhood on I'm used to doing several things at the same time. I always did homework in the living room at the wind-up table, while my mother was cooking in the kitchen and chitchatting with the neighbor. I listened, of course.

I had spent a quiet night with Tobi in the bedroom. Since he had to stay sober until 11 am, this measure was necessary. I had to lift him into the car suffering from back pain. Getting out was easy. Just on the way to the vet, Tobi ran right between my legs, and I fell. Murphy says hello. Another master, who also took over a chained dog, opened the door for me. I had to pull Tobi strongly. Then, I went to the post office sending letters to two birthday children. To get another bag of earth, I drove to the Plaza shopping center, where I bought a blackberry and a currant bush. When I balanced the sack and could not look at my feet, I fell over the rail of a forklift truck. The woman at the counter rushed to me: "Are you hurt?" I said: "Yes, but not from falling." Later I came again. She asked: "Are you okay?" I answered: "As good as one can be when hubby dies after 44 years." The woman left her place, came around to me and hugged me with comforting words remembering the incident when a friend asked me if I was going back to Germany. Another one said, what should she do there? Well, I hardly believe that one is embraced and comforted by total strangers. But who knows, Germans may have changed too.

3-19: In Vila Novo de Casela on the market, I bought two more cork bags from the woman I had gotten one together with Peter.

These are always beautiful gifts from Portugal where the cork oaks grow. In the restaurant where we usually eat, we spoke again about Peter. Today, the conversation was easy. Karl said: "When we briskly walked, Peter had to stop more often. In any case, we all would like to die like this, and it was Peter's wish as well, that's for sure." We all agreed and talked about our fear of long-time suffering above all having to live in an old-age home.

Renate came with Anna and the children to get to know Tobi. The dog seemed as fond of children as I expected and let himself be stroked extensively. It looked like he tried to keep Joshua from running away.

When picking weeds, I always have the bag Peter ordered on the Internet hanging around my neck with the mobile phone. When Mia and Tobi stood so sweetly side by side on the street, I wanted to take a picture. I entered the code and presto immediately the smartphone was ready for shooting. At first, I thought, Peter can now also fumble around with me on the mobile phone. Usually, the menu is displayed. It would have been time, since March 12, it is a broadcast pause. But then I remembered that Renate yesterday took a picture. I can already see a message from Peter in about every event that comes is breaking the ranks. Since he always only handled the mobile phone, it is still new to me.

3-21: After a shortened choir practice, we had our annual event in the Cafe Ze, where the repertoire, performances, finances, etc. were discussed. At 7:00 pm the invited Portuguese music group Veredas da Memoria appeared. Then we sang Rose of Tralee and Canção do Mar.

When we open up, we learn more

My highlight was Betty's long embracing. She said: "I'm sorry. It must be so hard for you". I said: It is the most difficult time I ever had to go through. But I have to be thankful. We had such a beautiful life and traveled all continents." Betty said, "yes, you can be pleased to have had such a lovely man." I enjoyed the Dutch woman's comment. After I'd talked about my post-mortal experiences with Peter, she told me about her brother who was in the hospital. She came from far away to visit him. It was already in the evening. The doctor said he's sleeping now, come in the morning. Betty blamed herself for not having insisted on an immediate visit, for her brother died that night. She sat next to him for all the following morning, holding his hand and speaking to him. Betty's sister-in-law asked her not to waste time. Not believing in the soul's continued life she thought, Betty would not achieve anything, Two or three years later, she had revised her opinion because her husband had appeared as spirit.

I do not know´ what it is that I often suffer from a pain in my right eye when staying for hours at Café Ze. Whether it is the neon lighting or the loud music or the food? So, as often before, I left as well as Wendy and Trixie. It took too long for them as well.

3-22: When walking the dogs the way I walked with Peter, my tears usually run down my cheeks.

3-24: Last night I dreamed of Peter. In a large house, we lay in bed naked as mother bore us. But we decided for another bedroom. We were just cuddling with each other when I woke up.

3-27: I´d dreamed that I was with a strange man in a pub dancing. After that, I was with Peter in a large open American road cruiser on vacation. The end of the dream: Peter drove quickly into the reverse gear to a gas station. I said in English to a woman that I had now just accustomed myself so beautifully after this one week, and already have to get away. The very last week with Peter was also particularly nice.

Today I felt pretty good all day. I collected wood, dug a beautiful wild lavender plant for Jochen's birthday. I also put one next to the roses to keep away the aphids. I can hardly believe that another year has passed. It occurred to me as a few months ago when I went to Jochen with Peter and the two big boxes of beer.

I had not cried a single time before 6 p. m. But some music or was it a certain sentence I had heard on a TV quiz, and suddenly it started again. I thought shortly before that I always wanted such a small farm and really have everything I want, except for Peter: a work I love, animals I love, the choir, friends, I can do everything now and watch the TV shows I like. Peter had recently asked twice what I was doing when he was not there. I said, "What I do now, just without you. But please, please, time. Stay put! "He said: "Oh, you'll soon find somebody else. "Nope, thank you. No need for old men. You're not old for me because I've grown old with you. But I can not imagine beginning a new life with an old man. Perhaps I will go before you. "Peter said: "I do not think so." I said:" Stay with me for a few more years. "Peter said: "Well, but this vein on my temple will burst someday." I said: "Why don't you see a doctor. Maybe it can be fixed. "Peter gave back: "But I do not want to grow old anyway."

Between 2:30 and 3:30 p. m. I enjoyed two pieces of fruit cake with cream and a cappuccino at Jochen's birthday party. At 7:30 pm, I had some cheese with sauteed aubergine and onions and a nut yogurt from the Minipreso, since I had no time before the choir to get organic yogurts. At 8:30 p. m. I had pulse rushing and extrasystoles. Or was it the choir? We sang the last song Sloop John B., today of all days where Trui was back! It was Ton's favorite song. Some choir members sang it at his deathbed. Ton died last December. When Trui went to the toilet, I knew at once that she was crying. Since the Beach Boys was also one of Peter's favorite bands, tears rolled down my cheeks again. It is quite hard, this grief work.

3-28: At about 6:30 a. m., I was at my yoga program and had to pee. I got up suddenly feeling very strange in my head. I thought now me too and called, "Peter am I joining you?" I noticed I had no panic whatsoever. Another advantage, if the partner goes, apart from the lost kilos, no more fear of dying.

Any more physical phenomena?

Yesterday, on March 3, I was particularly sad because Peter has not reported for a long time. At about 5:30 p.m. Uschi called on the fixed telephone from Germany. I asked, "Can you remember how Werner did make himself felt? I just remember he came from above and scared you in your sleep. "

Uschi said," Yes, I thought he was up to mischief, but later I realized that he wanted to remind me of my reflux problems. I should not sleep on the back because of the acid reflux, but on the left side, and because he came up to me from above, I realized that I was lying on my back. I remembered something else. I had taken my amber necklace in the evening and laid it on the table "... Uschi was gone. When she had called again, she said: "What was that?" "No idea. So, what about the chain? Uschi said: "In the morning it lay in a heart shape on the table. "Wow!" "Then something else. At the door, I have a fake orchid in a heavy planter. I was with Renee at the back of the room, when the pottery had just flown to the center. "... The telephone was dead again and immediately came to life. I asked: "What was it now?" "Do not know. What did you get? "That the pottery has landed in the middle of the room." Uschi said, "yes, and when I wanted to carry it back to its place, I found a fresh rose leaf directly underneath it!" I said, "maybe he had contacted Sai Baba." Gosh, this has never happened. Gone, again! When Uschi called again, I said, "maybe Peter wants you to call me on WhatsApp."

After two further attempts on the fixed line, Uschi rang me on WhatsApp on Peters mobile phone. I didn't know what was happening. Because the only time I had a call shortly after Peter's transition when the cellular suddenly lighted up. I saw Uli's name and moved to the blue arrow. But this time it was not so. I had to enter the code first. And then Uschi was already gone. But suddenly it was her turn, and the conversation was okay. Apparently, Peter wanted to show me that even then by his manipulation he'd enabled me to take the call from Uli without the code. Spirits consist of energy and can therefore easily interfere with electrical devices and influence them with their higher frequencies. I've already read about this in Jürgenson's "Voice Transmissions With The Deceased" (1996). I'm curious if Peter will ever call me on the phone. It is also possible to give calls from the beyond.

3-31: I feel better now because of yesterday's experience. Uschi's hair-raiser with the flower pot, by the way, was only a half year ago. I had asked Uschi if it was all right for her that Werner now and then announces, what she answered affirmatively. You are always advised to let go of the souls. But I am selfish at the moment, and I think the spirits know what to do with their far better perspective.

22.30: I zapped from a talk show to *Let's Dance* and regretted that I missed the best dance of Gil Ofarim. Switching channels I see the race track of Willow Springs, where Peter also several times raced his yellow MGB around the track. Well, at least something, maybe Peter comes more.

I'm calling "Peter, Willow Springs Raceway. The title 'Born 2 Race' reminds me of our red Cadillac convertible with the number HI42DAY where you were almost shot at the Mexican border because of this drug dealer number plate. I don't remember who you were with, probably with long-stay guest Bode and Borgmann. But the details are lacking. There I need your help. Perhaps you can transmit me everything as the otherworldly Billy Finger did for his sister. The film is almost over anyway then I can continue reading Annie Kagan's book. Oh, now comes 'Race 4 Glory'. Then I better wait until the witching hour, in 33 minutes. I'm about to fall asleep, and again I'm feeling your presence. Well, because the soul also leaves the body when sleeping it is free. Twelve minutes remaining. No TV-snow, no message. But without your help, I cannot write the book about the car dealership. If I only think of the beginnings in Hermosa Beach. I do not even remember the model of the ivory-colored Mercedes only that it had a suicide door. And you let the nice car roll against a post. After all, I remember buying and selling this car because the Jewish owner from San Diego did not believe you were no Jew. He wanted to give you a box of miniature hearing aids, but you refused. Well, at least then he recognized you are not a Jew since one would have taken the gift. Me, too. Maybe because my father had written Wilhelm Busch's poem in my poetry book:

Will das Glück nach seinem Sinn
Dir was Gutes schenken,
Sage Dank und nimm es hin
Ohne viel Bedenken.

Jede Gabe sei begrüßt,
Doch vor allen Dingen:
Das, worum du dich bemühst,
Möge dir gelingen.

Fortunately, despite the little mishap, we found a customer, a dentist from Aurich. He bought some other cars as well, but I know neither which nor how many. I was not involved in the purchase or sale of Yul Brynner's silver Gullwing and Grace Kelly's 190 SL. But oh well, the purchase of the red 300 SL I remember too, of course. I've attracted much attention from the other bidders by kicking the air. But you may not have gotten the car as cheap if I had not inspected the underbody and cursed. The other bidders may have become uncertain by my little show.

Sure, I had underestimated the value and was afraid you'd fool away. And then you made a profit and yet you sold it much too cheap because you did not know that it had an aluminum engine. Karl-Heinz Zepfel was aware of it and found it on the chassis number. He rubbed his hands after the purchase and can now retaliate with you. Isn't he already ten years in the afterworld? Maybe he has already learned a lot and can show you around."

Now, reading the books about the hereafter, I'm envious, perhaps the reason why many long-term life companions follow soon after losing their loved-ones. They also may read the grief-supporting books longing for their loved ones and the paradise conditions. And, since I know from the aftermath contacts of my cousins' husband that also suicides do not simmer in hell, I had even fancied this idea. But I would not commit suicide unless I'd suffer unbearable pain. I also think I may not have fulfilled my task here.

4-1: I have dreamed of Peter. We were driving somewhere on vacation, racing holiday? A young woman orders something and asks Peter to pay for it. He shows his arm, wearing a cheap watch paying anyway. In the figurative sense, he has not much but lends his last shirt. I dream of dresses unpacked from suitcases, the best I like is a light blue sweater. A garment signifies a mantling and defense of external influences. With a sweater, we cover the upper body while at the same time the heart is wrapped. The dream symbol "sweater" can express in this context that the dreamer wants to protect himself from emotional injuries.

http://traum-deutung.de/pullover/

Blue represents truth, wisdom, heaven, eternity, devotion, tranquility, loyalty and openness. Perhaps you are expressing a desire to get away. Definitely, yes! If you are wearing light blue in your dream, then it symbolizes your creativity. You like to pace yourself in whatever you are doing.

www.dreammoods.com/dreamthemes/colors.htm

If you see a watch in a dream shows and reminds you to have to divide your time better because you miss important things in your life. If you see other people wearing a watch in a dream announces huge success is approaching you.

http://dreamsnest.com/watch/

At the moment don't care if I will be successful. A few months ago, I would have liked the idea to have another bestselling book to buy a new scooter for Peter and a new motorhome. Many years ago, Peter used to wear expensive Rolex watches. From my first fee for my bestseller Spirulina, das blaugrüne Wunder I paid back my BAFöG (Federal Training Assistance Act) and bought Peter a beautiful Tag Heuer watch. But Peter had not worn a watch for a long time. These were not important to us anymore.

But one thing I learned by reading the dream interpretations since there were so many different ones: Paper doesn't blush.

4-9: Today I noticed that I did not write down everything strange happening with Peter. Because last week I was looking for my little egg spoon. I am very picky about it and guard it like gold. Peter sometimes teased me and put it on his plate. It even happened that I noticed it very late and I took the spoon in the middle of the meal out of his mouth. We laughed heartily at the attempt. That is why Peter has probably played this trick on me, to make me laugh again. It's nice that he kept his humor in the other world. I had done the dishes but had stowed them away only half a day after, my pet-spoon was gone, just gone. Although I knew it must have been in the sink, I looked for it in every possible place. For the next breakfast egg took another spoon, resigned to the fact that this must now be my favorite. When I was about to do the dishes again, my missing spoon was all alone gleaming in the sink!

"You probably wanted to use it again. And now you have another little joke on me to cheer me up: When working on the Cranberry book, I typed in the Google translator: In the end, the only left to be desired is to wish you all the best on your way to the light, to inner freedom, to serenity, and to radiant health! Thank you for your trust!"

Instead of the German translation, this came out:

In the end, all that's going to be, you're all right, you're right, you're right, you're right. Thank you for your trust!

"Yes, Peter, I hope you're right, that I'll catch up again at the end. You have always doubted a life after physical death. I've always said you'll see it. I am also glad that it is now really so that I was right."

Now I do it again with a new window: Yes, there it comes right:
Am Ende ist alles, was noch zu wünschen übrig ist, Ihnen alles

Gute auf Ihrem Weg zum Licht, zur inneren Freiheit, zur Gelassenheit und zu strahlender Gesundheit zu wünschen! Danke für Ihr Vertrauen!

"Well, Peter, if you go on like that, we'll have soon filled the book. I understand the message. You now know it too. You have always doubted that we continue to live on, just like my father. And who knows if you ever believed me back then when I told you every morning what my father had channeled me after his transition. "

I'd used to say you'll come to know it as well. Please, give me a sign then. And what a splendid sign of his otherworldly existence I got. He planned his whole funeral service with chorales and biblical quotations; they sounded in my inner ear: "I am with you always till the end of time","And behold, I am with you all the days, until the completion of the age." ... Every morning I woke up with another verse and a chorale. I was particularly receptive on the first day. On the eve of my father's transition, I knew nothing about the exact cause of his death. In the morning I awoke with the clairaudience of the Internationale. My mother immediately had an explanation. (Family Code page 163)

At the end of the election night, the members of the Social Democrats' party always sing the Internationale. My father's weak heart must have been overloaded with joy since, after 16 years of Kohl's agonizing government, SPD Chancellor Schröder could reign. Pa probably sang loudly and accidentally swallowed his partial prosthesis, for we did not find it anywhere.

After-death contacts via water, sausage, and teleportation

The magnificent crystal on the next page resembles the attic of a house. An eye on the left side of the roof looks at a rectangular object next to the recess.

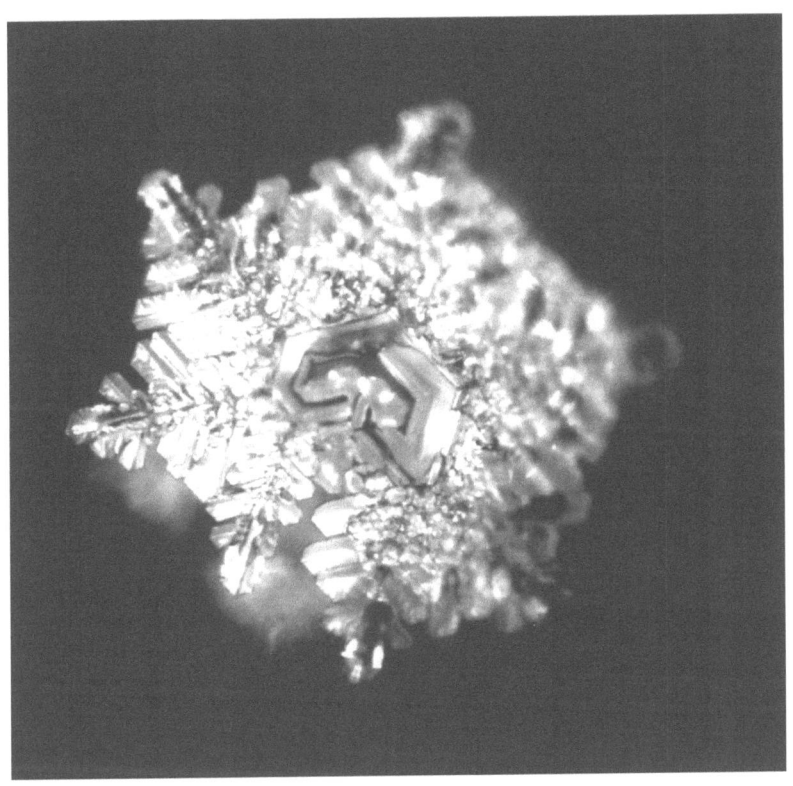

My mother went with me to the attic. Bending forward, I walked into the direction of a shelf. My mother exclaimed: "Yes, there, he has his paperwork." In one file I found manuscripts from the year 1951.

At this time I had other after-death contacts. We had invited our friends, Marianne and Helmut Müller for coffee, cake, and a round of Canasta. The two had hardly sat at the table when I felt the presence of my father. I was filled with love and almost burst with joy. Never before except for my near-death experience at the age of 21, I felt so much love and kindness. My father loved to play. Whether chess, skat, or Mau Mau, he was always ready for a game. Since I'd always asked him to give me a clear sign after his transition, he had repeatedly arranged things for me on the other side. In another experiment, I added to my handwritten name the question of whether my late father who had passed on and two recently deceased friends had something to tell. On the way to the post office to send the handwritten paper to the Atelier für Kunst und Mystik, I thought of my father asking him to give me a clear sign hoping for characteristic water crystals. Ernst F. Braun calls them soul star. But Pa did not want to wait that long as my readers can see reading the excerpt from my book Wasser - Code geknackt? Wasserkristallfotos: Bildersprache der Seelen:

I walked with my husband to the post office to send the slip with the question to the deceased. In my mind, I was with my father and asked him to give me a clear sign. On the way back, my gaze fell on an advertising poster with sausages. Though I use to avoid sausage, a compelling force made me enter the shop where the nice German-Russian usually sells me Siberian cranberries.

Following an inner urge, I pointed to a poultry salami and two more sausages. With a full plastic bag, I left the shop under the delighted and amazed stares of my husband. After climbing the Kisselberg, we sat down on the edge of the fountain to rest.

Suddenly, I had an intense craving. I said let's try the salami. Throwing all the hygienic concerns overboard, Peter pounded around with the key at the salami. I said: Hopefully, no one will come by now thinking about one of my readers, which I often met. He is on the road almost every day. A fraction of a second later, the latter hastened past us. I exploded with laughter. What is going on here? Then, in a quiet moment, the scales fell from my eyes. Had I not asked my father for a clear sign? But I thought about one via water crystal photos. Has my old man arranged this all so amusingly? At first, he transferred me his immense desire for sausage and then sent the health-conscious man the moment I thought of him. Thank you, Pa, for your imaginative cooperation! (Meyer, 2008)

I remember something remarkable. At the funeral of my father, I came into contact with Marlene Asensio from Fränkisch-Crumbach. We talked about our hobby cycling and arranged for a small tour. Since Peter and I wanted to buy a new sofa set at that time, I had a brochure from the furniture store Kempf and asked Marlene to stop by there. Marlene was wearing a cyclist outfit. She stowed the leaflet in her pocket on the back. We talked about this and that, time passed. Suddenly, Marlene moved strangely and said, "What is that?" The brochure jumped up out of her pocket and landed on the bench on which we sat! "Oh," I said, "we almost forgot. We must hurry, they'll close in half an hour."

14-4 at 9.00: I just answered a WhatsApp message from Loni, who always calls Peter's cell phone. When I was about to send the greetings to the whole family, the son had also come from Bavaria for Eastern, it didn't go through. I tried several things. Suddenly I saw a self-taken picture of Peter. I added it as an attachment and bada bing then it went through. Was Peter involved in it?

Mandira asked me how I was doing. At 11:01 a. m., I'd send her an e-mail: "It's a bit better now. The weather is also very nice. Peter gets in touch at odd times with little surprises, sometimes quite funny. Well, he took his humor into the other world. Still, in the flesh, I got little help with the books. Now he even wants to work with me on them. Sounds crazy, huh? I have a firm program now:

In the morning at 10:00 after the dog feed has sat down and I've cleaned up I walk the dogs, also at around 6 p. m. Tuesdays choir, Saturdays market, followed by a café visit for the company. Soon I'm going to start a once a week visit the dog beach.

11.45: Just as I finished writing I'm better, I cried again. The best would be to say nothing anymore. It can also be that Doris Day's songs, I just listen to, are too sentimental at the moment, or because it is Good Friday. I don't know.

4-17: Yesterday the kids had come, Peters little grandniece and grandnephew, to find their Easter bunny. The adults refreshed themselves on the Nispero tree, which Peter had cut back a few months before. And again, I forgot to ask Delio or Jochen to re-close the French Door. Meanwhile, I have succeeded doing it with a knife. It suddenly occurred to me: a thought transfer?

18.00: I just wanted to fill the hydraulic oil in the Xantia, opened the lid of the new bottle, and immediately got angry because the float was visible´correctly between the two lines. So it could not have been the problem, but it was this kind of noise. And again a déjà vu, I was aware of this scene because I had already dreamed it. I was upset before that I opened the bottle for nothing.

4-18: I've planted four bushes and hope I'll have besides oranges, tangerines, and Japanese plums also the more expensive berries next year. Two blueberry bushes and a currant, gooseberry, and a raspberry bush. Hopefully, they will ever bear fruits. So far this year everything else has blossomed beautifully.

I watch the story of my life at VOX. Rebecca Mir and Maximo Sinató, the couple who had met at Let's Dance. They worry about their age if one remains alone. Rebecca says Massimo's father was married for 46 years and has no desire to find a new wife. I also

46

think it is hard to reflect about another partner if one has spent most of life together with one. The moderator, Désirée Nosbusch, asked Massimo what he would say to Rebecca if he knew he had only a short time to live. He would tell her that he had enjoyed every moment and did not regret a single minute and that they would meet again. "I am so grateful that you have entered my life and made me the happiest man in the world."

Peter's words were very similar in the last week(s) of his earthly life. What would have happened if he had told me he would not live a long time? My nights would have been sleepless, filled with despair and fear. I cried again, at the thought of how Peter's nights might have been. On his birthday, he was strikingly calm and had been eating and drinking less than usual.

I will read the book On Life After Death by Elisabeth Kübler-Ross again, where the psychiatrist describes her perceptions, which she had with dying, very authentic (2012).

Do we know when our time comes?

Something is strange: As in California in the late 1980s, I had ordered an Astro chart in English and a day's horoscope by e-mail half a year ago. I guess I had dreamed prophetically of Peter's transition but quickly suppressed it. The sentence of the separation from a loved one I'd read already before February 11, but where? Perhaps in a dream. But with bad news, we people like to use the defensive mechanism of suppression.

Von: **Astroportal** <noreply@web01.astroportal.com>
Datum: 11. Februar 2017

Hello Ms. Meyer,

Below you will find your day horoscope for today

Love & Partnership

There might be a separation from a loved one. It weighs heavily on you. If fate wants it, you will meet each other again. But you should leave it to chance. It can not be forced.

Well, I should leave it to chance, though I would like to be with Peter. Life without the tiresome body is so much easier. For as happy as I met Peter in his new home, I was indeed envious when I was back in my bed.

Peter probably knew his time had come. He said on January 11, on the official opening of the Elbphilharmonie in Hamburg, "I will not see it in this life anymore, you well may." He also had our whole life reviewed and behaved differently than usual. Peter was much more compliant. He often told me he loved me and I was his best woman ever. He also had revealed his happiness about the many beautiful things we had experienced together and that these memories cannot be taken from us. Days before his sudden death, he said, "I am so glad and grateful that you have come into my life. "I always thought I was a jinx, but having been with you was a real stroke of luck." I think Peter had foreseen his demise just as much as my father, who did not write on his annual folders, as in the previous years 1996 and 1997, but instead until the end of September 1998. On October 1, 1998, he had left his body.

Perhaps Peter's friend Bolko has already prepared him via gray letters in TV snow. For when we saw that phenomenon together after midnight about two weeks premortal, he said nothing about my commentary on the spirit message. Since only on rare occasions I am awake at this time, and Peter was up almost every night until about 2 a.m., it could be that he had without me deciphered the letters and he possibly already knew what Bolko had so important to tell him. Maybe we all get a message from the Grim

Reaper when it is our time. Marita had seen a black woman in a black limousine. Just a couple of weeks before 9-11, 2001, where Marita collided with a truck one hour before the collapse of the WTC towers, we were playing golf at the Sansenhof in the Oden- wald. Marita had told me about her dream where she was sitting in a black sedan. When turning her head, she saw a woman all in black on the back seat. In Erbach, we looked at the Tutankhamun exhibition and drank something on the terrace. At the same time, she put all her jewelry off and asked me for a reiki treatment. I felt a vibration. In the evening we ate at the *Brasserie*, and in the boudoir, in front of the ladies' room, Marita wanted another chan- neling of the universal energy. When we said goodbye, she got out of the car and hugged me long and deeply. It was obviously a farewell. I do not remember whether it was in this or the follow- ing night when I dreamed of the collapse of the towers and Marita's accident. I only remember the fact that I told Peter about my dream and said to him: "I saw on TV the towers of the World Trade Center collapsing, but it did not seem like a movie, that was real, and then I was dreaming that Marita had a deadly accident with a truck. "

With Theo it was similar. Just before we went back to the south with the camper, my goddaughter Andrea came with Theo and the children. Theo said: "I'm not going to get much older. I better stop working soon." We did not know how to react to the young man's words. In the night I dreamed of Theo's accident, in which he also collided with a truck. I mentioned it to my mother who reacted outraged. Heide, Andrea's mother, said: "Yes, Theo lately has talked a lot about that he'd been lucky in life, but now he'd have no more guarding angels. I still remember the zombie-like face expression of Andrea standing in front of the chapel and looking with her young children after the leaving funeral car. In our family,

49

we have experience with sudden losses of our loved ones. Andrea has also offered assistance. I was moved by all the concern and the offers, to talk or to shop together. I was also delighted to get invitations for a children birthday and a dance performance. Renate also told me about other widows who meet regularly. She thought I might want to join them.

I think most people have a sense of their death. Peter's mother seemed to be quite certain at the end of the 1980s when we visited her in Wilhelmshaven.

Lisa talked a lot about death. Decidedly, she ordered us not to make a fuss. I do not want a ceremony, you hear, plant the urn, and that's it. Peter seemed to feel uncomfortable in his skin. Because his 76-year-old mother complained of no health problems, he said: "Oh, mommy, do not think of dying, you will still survive us all." Peter calmed himself more than his mother, who steadfastly continued, "Peter gets the serving cabinet, Joachim the car." I had never experienced my mother-in-law so expressly. Before that, she'd talked about her death. On Omi Köster's funeral, she pathetically said, I'll be next. This time it sounded different. Family Code, p. 87 f.

4-21: Yesterday Karl-Dieter called again because of the 6,3 and the truck. He asked, among other things, how Jochen is. KD himself had lost his younger brother. I said: "Jochen lost weight like me, that's normal when mourning. And he seems to be worried stiff, for he has spared no expense and arranged for a full physical examination. For me, it is the reverse. My health is now less important to me. And, since my children are also on the other side, what should prevent me from exchanging the vale of tears for the already observed paradise conditions? Maybe just the books Peter wants to write with me to awaken the people who may change their view of life and lose their fear of death.

On April 22, Peter probably made me realize that I do not have to write a cranberry book in German anymore. It seems that spiritual children can also have a fighting spirit and do not always as their parents want. On that day I released my cranberry book in English for printing. In the evening I wanted to start with the German edition. Most of the prelims I use to copy from the just manufactured books. But this time it did not work. The copied pages disappeared again and again. I thought, well, I'm supposed to take a break. The next morning I woke up with the thought that I was able to see ghosts living in Hermosa Beach, California. Would it help to imitate the living conditions of the idyllic Pacific community? We stayed at Apartment 11 on Ardmore Ave. 1820 = cross total 11. From Lynne Palmer, I learned that in houses with the number 11 or cross total 11 there was an increase in supernatural experiences. At that time, "I searched around the Library Department of donated books. When I reached for automatic writing, I found a brochure by Lynne Palmer. The title Your Lucky Days & Numbers had aroused my curiosity. The astrologer writes, in a house with the number or digit sum 11 the chances of experiencing the occult is great. " (ibid. p. 20).

So the first thing I went about was to cut two ones for the 11 from black tape and stuck them onto the front door. Outside onto the water clock box, I stuck a 7 and the 4, mine and Peters fate number, resulting in the cross total 11. Now I'm curious to see if my sensory perception will work as well again, as in Hermosa Beach.

On April 23 in the morning after breakfast and walking the dogs, I attempted to start with the German edition of the cranberry book. But again and again, it didn't work out though I decided to start all new. Even this didn't work out. Well, well I guess I do not need to write the cranberry book at all. Anyway as a Sagittarius I prefer writing new books instead of translating my works into another language. Turning to Peter's book and lo and behold, now I could copy and paste the title pages of the last written book.

Later I went outside to do some gardening. The raging storm had torn off four main branches of our trees. Some flower beds were smashed. I began to cut off the smaller branches from the first of the thick ones. I laid the stripped branch aside turning to the next one. Huh? All the branches were snapped. The interfaces were still close to each other. I said: "Well, Peter, are you still managing your tasks or are the brownies for real? " During the gardening, I thought of something else. My bedspread always looks like shaken out. About a week before Peter went into the light, he came to my bedroom for our morning kiss and straightened out my twisted bedding. Two-thirds usually concentrated in the lower third of the cover. Peter said: "I should shake it every week." It seems he did it for the last few months. It was always unusually perfect. Since Feb 11, the content of my bedding is always evenly distributed. I noticed that only recently, but the capped branches made the mental connection.

4-24: I had just checked on Facebook. A Patrizia marveled my comment that I'd like to write a new biography about Doris Day with emphasis on her work for animals. I let her know that after finishing Beyond Death, I'd contact Doris. Then I got up and made a vegetable broth. When I went back to the PC, the screen showed the cover of my cranberry book in English! During his lifetime, Peter hardly took care of advertising my books. Does he remind me now that I can mention it? "Gonna do it in a bit. You do not believe how I am pleased with your little attention. THANK YOU, Bobby!"

4-25: After the day of wasting (I had twice forgotten the water boiler on the stove), the night of many dreams followed. In one, Peter and I have entered the apartment of our neighbor's friends and went to their bed. Then I dreamed of my new, beautiful apartment. It was light and bright and decorated in gold tones.

Marianne E. Meyer

CRANBERRY POWER FRUIT

Handbook to the Methuselah Berry

Sensational Healing Successes and Delicious Recipes for the Healthy Kitchen

4-26: At the moment, I am very selfish and glad Peter is still with me. The more so as he said to Isa: I'll wait. It is, however, difficult. Strangely enough, the water crystal photo on the cover back informed by Peter's photo from page 12 shows the dog that came to me a few days after Peter passed on. Tobi can be seen on the bottom in the profile holding a kind of boomerang.

Next year, I'm going to ask Ernst Braun to make another test by informing neutral water with a signature from Peter. I hope I find one. He has thrown away so many papers that there are almost only mine left also proofing that Peter has known about his passing.

Today it was difficult. We sang with our choir again in the old people's home, where Peter had filmed and photographed last year and talked to a senior woman who was still there.

The work helps: I cut trees and bushes, water the plants, pluck weeds. The gardening is good work, and the two dogs keep me busy walking, the cats'meow in front of my bedroom window wakes me up in the morning. I have enough distraction.

4-27: I'd just uploaded the title page for our first joint book at BoD in German to see if the frame I see in the document is gone after uploading. Though the frame of the pic is gone, the photo has expanded. "Peter, getting out of line fits you perfectly. On our last photo, just eight months ago, you are as mellow beaming and happy looking as I've seen you in your new world. I miss you! I look strange on this photography."

Do we create our disasters by the word?

On April 28, Loni and Karl did visit me with their son. They went with me to eat at Restaurante Luis do Prego. I had baked a healthy cake, with coconut powder, chia seeds, and Nispero fresh from the tree, sweetened with stevia, which we enjoyed as a dessert with freshly ground coffee.

Sigrid also came because she needed the Amazon data for a complaint. Her new laptop had stopped working. I offered to borrow her my second laptop. Unfortunately, she did take it only later. Otherwise, I'd have had at least this one still functioning after next day's electric problem. I said to Loni, "Why did you come today? I wrote to you that it looks like rain, but the weather on Saturday

would be better. "Loni said," I wrote you that we are coming today. " „Where? I haven't found anything on Skype, Facebook or
Gmail. "Yes, I'm still only working with this tiny device. I said, "I
can not understand that. Do you have too much time? The writing
takes a lot longer because you're mistyping permanently. I also
only take the Samsung with me, Peter's heavy cellular always lying around at home. I do not like the whole stuff. It has always
been Peter's thing. For me, it is just a waste of time. Sometimes I
wish to return to the Stone Age. After all, I was a shepherd boy in
my last life. "I would have better not said that. Because in the
evening I had the Stone Age together with some neighbors. The
power cable lay in the middle of the road. Vis-à-vis the Monte
Oliva farm holiday had just guests who were standing in the
driveway. I called the electricity plant (Edp) around 7:30 p. m. re-
porting the problem. At about 10 p. m. I heard the noise of the
working electricians, going on until five o'clock in the morning,

only about ten meters from my bedroom window. When I wanted to turn on the news in the morning, nothing was working except for the light. Then I wanted to write an e-mail. But the laptop was not loading. I called Edp and told Philipp Vilena that neither W-LAN nor receiver or laptop work. The Samsung smartphone was empty. I plugged the charger into the multiple sockets. It hissed, I quickly pulled it out again. I realized that we must have gotten heavy current. Unfortunately, too late. All the other chargers, for the second laptop, the tablet and the other cell phone, all broken. During the day, I noticed two destroyed light bulbs. The old ones remained okay. Only the new expensive ones were gone. I then called again at Edp telling Pedro Forsica that the workers have probably laid power lines since the light is brighter than usual. He promised someone would come to me in the next four hours. I of course waited, but also after 18:00 clock nobody had appeared, though the light was normal again. When I switched on the large computer, nothing happened, only the screen still worked.

I drove to the Chinese to get light bulbs and a replacement charger for the Thinkpad. The receiver, which I bought at Warten electrical equipment market, could not be connected. It only works for Portuguese television. Fortunately, I still remembered the TV technician, with whom we sent the e-bike a second time. The first time we did send it via post office. After three weeks we had a notification in the box to pick up the bike. They cannot send it to Germany because of the lithium battery. But the battery was marked on the transmission form. On the carton, a huge e-bike with the battery was pictured and yet the ladies at the post office took it. How should I have known that they don't send bikes with batteries? But the stunner is still coming: After more than a year, I did not get my €118 payment back. That's why I'm not exactly op-timistic about getting a penny from Edp. At José, a nice man in a wheelchair, I bought a charger for my Asus. Together with the repair of the receiver and the big PC I paid a total of €74. With the smartphone cost of €169 and some chargers and light bulbs, the total damage was around €270. Edp offered €37 but need some more papers and forms filled out. I think I forget about it. For me writing about my feelings when I get a raw deal serves me as an outlet. Why wasting time for an uncertain outcome?

While walking the dogs, at a nearby rubbish dump I discovered a pile of coarse sand or small stones. Every day I carried two plastic bags full of home-towed, sieved and laid with Sigrid's cement marble break with it. She had just finished a construction project and brought me her remaining cement.

Again and again, I think this entire thing I have put on myself, as I also explained in the book Family Code in Chapter: Are We the Creator of Disasters? Here an example:

During my coffee withdrawal depression in 1987, I had often thought, it would be best to crash together with my mother ... I had even mentioned this in letters to friends.

In fact, in the night just before our flight, I dreamed of a plane dipped in white smoke and woke up sweating. Peter said, "that's just an anxiety dream." But in another dream, I asked Peter to cancel the flight. I also wanted to stop my mother from flying, but she did not believe me. She thought Peter would have persuaded me because we had so much work with the classic cars. It was the first time we had stayed at the window watching the LH jumbo taking off and disappearing into the distance. After an hour, we had just looked at a blue pagoda, Peter said, "now Alwine will be flying over Las Vegas." I had a queasy feeling and said, "who knows where she is now."

In our neighboring village Manhatten Beach we enjoyed the happy hour at Orville & Wilbur and the sunset with hot live music. The free snacks, if you ordered a drink, saved us dinner. I handed the raw vegetables with dip, stuffed eggs, and tuna pizza. Peter still had 2-3 shrimp and oysters for small cash. Arriving home the phone rang at about 7:00 p.m.

Peter picked up the receiver calling "Alwine!" It was just as I had dreamed. We drove to Westchester.

All passengers were accommodated at the Amfac Hotel near LAX airport. 15 minutes later, I was greeted by my mother in the crowded conference room: "You white witch! You were dead right", she said cheerfully. "And I did not believe you. Sit down beside me. I have kept the seats free for both of you." Some passengers were aware of my latest prophecy. I was almost greeted like a pop star. After this experience, I realized crystal clear:

**If we are agitated or the body is lacking nutrients,
it has an impact on the whole. We create our reality
through thinking, speaking and writing.
We are causing global catastrophes,
and that is why we take responsibility
for all the life around the world.
Therefore it should be desired to live with happy people.
My experience shows us clearly, how we are all connected.
We're all sitting in the same boat.**

Or in the same plane. The rich and most powerful people depend on what even the poorest think and feel. Increasing disasters and burn-outs indicate a lot of negative stimuli. Depression can cause destruction. That is why we should be interested in making other people happy! Is this not the true meaning of life? Since this experience, I have been thinking that I am not sending any unreflected requests into the ether.

If the tongue reacts faster than the brain, we are better cautious or silent. Because: Loose lips sink ships and crash aircraft. (Family Code, p. 84 f.)

Unfortunately, in my exceptional situation, I once again thought about something and catapulted me into the Stone Age.

It was strange to see my mother's first visit to the US that on her very first day she was as close to the transition to the hereafter as she was last.

Still more after-death contacts

Ma came just before Peter's birthday. Long before dawn, I heard her bustling about in the kitchen. I groped for my glasses, sat up, and walked drowsily to her. She held her forearms under the faucet and let cold water run over them. A pot of water stood on the gas flame. Is it the jet lag? I looked at the clock: It's only 5!

Jesus, that was close. My mother's dramatic voice alarmed me. What's wrong with you? I forgot my heart tablets twice. Why? Since flying west, it was never dark. I did not think of it, she said with a forgiving smile! Tzzz! And how was that? I could not feel my pulse anymore. Do you know how I noticed it was serious? Huh? I dreamed I was in Schönbrunn in the house of a childhood friend. In the dream, I have seen beautiful oval picture frames. People danced and laughed. They've lured me to come. Ma made the typical sign with the pointing finger. Suddenly I realized that they were all dead relatives and acquaintances. But funny, my friend still lives (2 months later we learned that she had actually died). I said, no, not now, not here with Marianne. I pulled myself together ... oh, Jesus, that was by a hair. (Family Code p. 17 f.

Since the recent television experiences with Peter and my mother making me aware of certain programs, I think the

59

following happening was probably orchestrated by my deceased father 16 years ago, and not a strange coincidence. At that time, in the late evening of the 24-hour race at the Nürburgring in 2001, I was sitting in front of the TV, as Peter was one of those warhorses turning night into day to race through the Green Hell. Zapping in the commercial break to a Western on channel Kabel 1, I was astonished seeing John Hudson in a close-up kneeling position with a cowboy hat and a gun. It was the first time I saw our friend in a movie, before only in series, one time with Larry Hagman and his bottle spirit Barbara Gordon, but never in a Western. As if that was not enough, the first announcement of another Western with the two main actors Jocelyn Brando and Montgomery Clift came immediately after the end of the movie. That was very strange, two friends and Peter the same night on TV! I immediately called and said, "I just see you in a white-brown striped dress. How can that be, you John and Peter on the same evening on the TV? "Jocelyn said,"you may find out." Yes, but it took some years. That was probably Pa.

In the afternoon after the funeral, my father could also have had his spiritual hands in the game or guided the Cameraman's hands. I was expected at the Windpferd publishing house at the Frankfurt Book Fair to present my books and to offer drinks with Spirulina and treats. *According to the motto, the show must go on Peter drove me to Frankfurt after the ceremony and the funeral feast. And as the needle in the haystack, my mother saw me on TV walking in one of the corridors looking for the Windpferd stall.* (ib. p. 144)

Our tomcat Max also had an after-death contact about 14 years ago. He came screaming in a panic to the terrace door. Howling, he raced through the apartments, as if a ghost had followed him. On this day we learned: It was not just a saying: Our landlady had left her fleshly body at that time in the hospital. Mrs. Peters had often spoiled Max with fat treats who rewarded her with his cute presence. Max, who was very shy with most people, came to me as the only one of our 14 velvet paws. He came again in from the terrace door screaming. I thought he was in pain and took him to the veterinarian. But an hour later at home in my arms, Max took his last deep breath without any suffering. Then he vibrated briefly all over his body making me realize that we are electric beings increasing the frequency after physical death.

I'm looking at Peter's water crystal photo on the back of the book cover. Ernst F. Braun was so kind to give me this soul star as he calls it. I had sent him Peter's photo. Mr. Braun had placed a bottle of distilled water on it for three days, then he took drops, froze them, and microscopically photographed them at -5 degrees. Before, I did not notice the light bulb, northwest of the dog with the black boomerang. But after the heavy-current disaster, I think that this was also a prophecy, just as when my deceased father had predicted the encapsulation of my mother and her severe depression via stone face and cocoon. At that time Ernst Braun informed the distilled water only with the note on which I wrote my name and the question to my father if he had something to tell me.

Since my mother did not want to drive anymore after a small car accident, she was cut off from all her activities, such as singing, dancing, gymnastics and honorary activities. She pulled back more and more. But sometimes when I went with Peter from our hill to the Old Town, she also walked down into the town from her hill on the opposite side. She said she had suddenly an urge to get dressed and go. We then both thought of Pa, that he probably arranged our meeting masterfully.

61

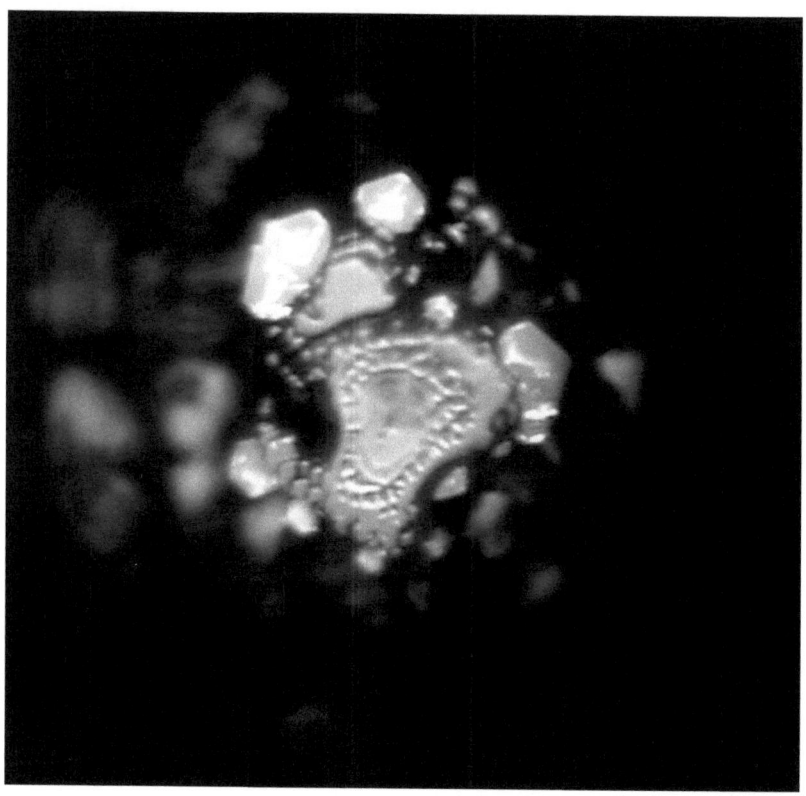

Nevertheless, my mother's depression, perhaps connected with her high drug consumption and her borreliosis, could not be stopped anymore. I would have liked to rent a larger centrally located apartment and take Ma to me. But she did not want to give up her accustomed environment.

5-4: I'm almost a week without television. The repaired receiver shows a light but still signifies NO SIGNAL. Haven't I connected the cables properly? Can this also have to do with the LNB? Could it be the antenna is not properly aligned? Perhaps the satellite dish has shifted conditioned by the wind. Google advises realigning the dish horizontally and vertically. "Peter, I miss you and long for you everywhere I look."

Tomorrow I'll drive with Sigrid to Spain. Six days without TV. Perhaps I've already withdrawal symptoms because today I was quite distracted.

In the late afternoon, Renate took me to dance performances, where Annelie participated. At first, the 4 and 5-year-olds appeared. There was a cute red-haired chubby stage hog. She did her thing perfectly well and reminded us both of Corinna, one of Renate's schoolgirls, with whom I had also worked.

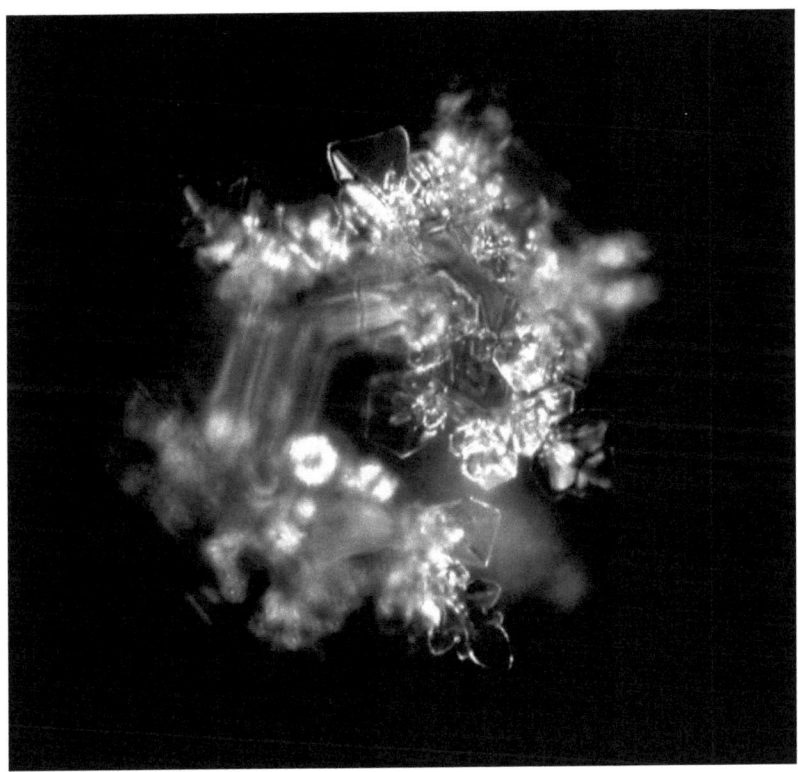

5-6:. The Saturdays are difficult for me. I light candles every Saturday afternoon. I was just calling Heide. She barely asked me how I was when the connection terminated. Was that Peter? Does he not want me to cry? After getting ready for the market, I called Heide again. We talked for a while. I was about to ask if she would miss her Karl if he dies before her, even though they live separately. There was no question as the conversation broke off. I guess I should not think about such things.

5-8: Since the flat screen TV still has the warranty, I grabbed it and drove to Olhao. The kind young women laughed at my acting talent. I mimicked what it is like to see only the picture, the moving mouths, and hear absolutely nothing. They promised to inform me within 48 hours whether the TV is repairable or I get a new one. I then chose a refrigerator and took measurements.

5-9: I put Peter's photo back on the couch. I do not know if it has anything to do with it, but after three months it seems to be worse. About two weeks ago I set the photo against the casket in the little lounge. Earlier, I already had one or two days without tears, but now no dry day anymore. It could also have to do with the fact that I had a neutral topic with the cranberry book and now I am mostly working with Peter. But the German cranberry book version was blocking me so to speak, as the copied title pages repeatedly disappeared signalizing that I only have to write Peter's book. Maybe then my purpose this time around will be fulfilled, and I can join Peter on the other side. I think we are all born with a task. I have already written about twenty books. Perhaps after this, I will be freed from my assignment. But as long as I do not know, I'll continue writing.

5-11: I caught a cold again. Right after the shock three months ago I had for many weeks a long-lasting cough, now I have a running nose and a scratchy throat from the many sneezes. Today of all days, invited by Uli for dinner! I was so happy yesterday when I suggested going to the Indian because Claudia ís a vegan. I wondered all day whether I should rather cancel, but as soon as the two arrived, the violent attack of sneezing took a break! When Claudia hugged me, I cried again and said, I had not imagined it to be so hard. After the delicious Indian food with red wine, we went to a cafe next door. We had a lot of fun, and when they had delivered me at home as if by command the sneezing started again until the throat was sore. I then found out that it hurts less when I sneeze into my mouth firmly closed.

5-12: I have not heard anything on the TV yet. Yesterday I called but spoke only on the answering machine. I guess I'm going to skip the idea of buying a refrigerator there. With this kind of poor service, I'd rather buy one in Tavira. Fortunately, José gave me an old TV I can keep as long as the regulation takes. I'll give him my Family Code book. On Monday, I'll put some oomph into it if I feel well again.

5-14: The cold is almost gone, but I do not feel well, though I've dreamed of Peter. Most my pants are too big. I sewed most of them tighter, some with darts. I went twice with the doggies, fetched some sand and cemented some marble pieces again. After I called cousin Heide, I felt better.

5-18: For two days the crying has subsided considerably. I can now be happy since I know I'm expected on the other side, where there is neither pain nor hunger or thirst, neither sweat nor freeze. Just how long will I have to wait?

5-20: Conforama has still not called. They have not even answered my e-mails only asked for the phone number but never called. Then, on a somewhat more massive e-mail, I finally got a call: The employee said it was in the guarantee conditions that Conforama have 30 days to repair the TV. Why not right away? I got the call while protecting the new camper tires from the sun. I wanted to get in but didn't find my keys. They must have fallen from my shirt pocket while covering the new tires of the motor-home with the cardboard. I ripped down the cardboard and removed the weeds around the camper. I also looked around the place where I had just recently heaved a large potted plant fallen from the storm to the neighbor. Nothing.

I managed to drag me to call Bolko's sister Freuke. Since Bolko had contact with his late brother Harro, I thought his sister might be psychic, too. But I spoke only with an answering machine.

5-21: The phone came to life. On a Sunday morning! "Adrian," said a voice. Who is that I thought and said, "yes, please, what can I do for you?" Mr. Adrian said: "You want to speak to Freuke." I said, "yes, right." He said: "That's not possible." I asked: "Why not?" "Freuke died a year and a half ago."

"Oh, I'm sorry." That is why Bolko only shrugged when I asked him thru Isabel if I should tell her about the channeling. I suppose he thought it would be good for Freuke's widower if I tell him. He said he couldn't help me. I should better call Tammo. Bolko's brother might have something to say to me.

It was again a beautiful Sunday with the flea market group in Vila Novo de Casela. Franz did not talk too much about his Cuba journey. It seems to have become quite expensive for tourists, even though a doctor earns only €40 a month. Everything is as expensive as it is here, but the hotels cost much more.

After the market, we went to Cacela Velha for food and climbed the hill to take another look at the easternmost lagoon of Ria

Formosa. After that, I was with Sigrid in the Robinson Club rummaging around in their boutique. We would almost have played table tennis. But I had to urgently pee. Since I didn't find a toilet and didn't want to ask as a non-member, we postponed it to next time.

5-22: The key stuck between two of my knitted pillows.

Trying to call Tammo Seifert, Bolko's brother, I have only reached the answering machine. Since I was looking for an e-mail address on the Internet, I found out that Tammo had written two biographies. I will encourage him to exchange books. His two books seem to be quite exciting. He got five stars from a former pupil named Thorsten Böhme who wrote a review: *I was not aware my former teacher in Latin and history (it's been a long time ...) is such a writing talent (heads off!!!). I have enjoyed this book: Memories of my own youth in Wilhelmshaven, the Max Planck school, friends, and the vacation home stay on Wangerooge have been awake.*

Since I would probably be able to visit Wangerooge in two months and see where Peter spent some time of his youth, I would like to read the book *Kino, Kirche, Kugeln aus Stahl: Eine Wilhelmshavener Kindheit in den 50er Jahren.*

On May 24 at 4:30 a. m. I woke up to an unknown shrill ringing noise. What was that? Huch, like the princess on the pea, I lay on something hard. Reaching under my behind, I pulled out the small plastic bottle with my eye drops. Right, yesterday after the choir rehearsal, I had slight pain in the right eye again and then forgot to drop my eyes. "Thank you, Peter, if that was you. But my bedspread I must shake myself again for about a week. I guess you

67

have more important things to do. Maybe working with Nikola Tesla on his aether energy powered car I presented in the water book."

I am just wondering what the meaning of my lack of smell and taste is. I'll try to get rid of Peter's T-shirt and shirt the ambulance men had cut into pieces.

Is everything written in the stars?

What is the purpose of astrology? Bolko, who was born in the same delivery room, half an hour before Peter has lived the same way as Peter up to the middle adult age. And both suddenly departed from the earth plane while walking. Both had married at the young age of 19, and both their wives got two sons. Both were divorced and lived in cohabitation for seven years before they married a second time. Ilse then got her son Konrad. Mine, Jan Jasper, had not made it to the earthly plane. Both, Bolko and Peter, were much too lax with money. Bolko had given away lots of gifts. Peter had lent way too much money. I just found a note with Peter's handwriting: "I'm here four years, and every month it should be paid. Berthold has talked me into giving him 2,000 and ...". The rest I could not decipher. Shortly before Peter's death, we talked about Berthold and Rudi Neidt, who also did not pay back the borrowed money.

At the end of their lives, which both Bolko and Peter lived to the fullest one thing was not as full as it used to be: their wallet.

Reading Henry Miller's book Big Sur and the Oranges of Hieronymus Bosch when he described his life in Big Sur, I often thought of my brother. Henry handled his children like Heini his Andreas. Their similar lifestyle, the radical individualism. At the end of the book, I discovered that the two not only have the same names, Henry and Heinrich. Miller was also born like my brother on December 26th. Both paint and write.

Or let's take for instance the two world stars, Marlon Brando and Doris Day. I read both biographies because I was a friend of Marlon's sister Jocelyn and am related to Doris. I have discovered insightful parallels:

On March 3, 1924, a girl in Cincinnati, Ohio, first saw the light of day. An hour before midnight that day 700 miles away, a boy was born in Omaha, Nebraska. Both suffered from the neglect of one or both parents. Both children were 12 years old when their parents divorced. The boy's hurting soul hidden behind a youthful macho behavior expressed in his early youthful rebel movie roles. The girl could sublimate emotional insecurity and insults already as a teenager by dancing and singing. For both, the close contact with their animals was a psychological support. Later both sought consolation in the faith in Mary Baker Eddy's Christian Science. As children, both aimed at a dancer's career but became convincing actors. Both had the gift of having to listen to a song only 1-2 times to be able to recite it. When they became world stars, they could not get used to the fuss about their fame. They were not interested in the rules of Hollywood and were considered social outsiders. Both were not interested in money and had left their dough with the biggest money-grubbers in their vicinity. Marlon gave it to his father, Doris to her husband. Both wannabe Dagobert's invested the money earned by their loved ones in cattle, soil treasures and other phony investments. Since they were secret-mongers in financial matters, the bereaved did not know if they "stashed away" assets, perhaps on Swiss number accounts.

Doris Day and Marlon Brando have made 39 movies each. In an English biography of David Kaufman, I read that Doris would have liked to work with Marlon. In 1968, in her second last movie, "Where Were You When the Lights Went Out?" it almost happened. For alongside Burt Lancaster and Richard Burton was Marlon Brando under consideration. But in the film, you can see that Doris was also happy with her partner Patrick O'Neal.

By this analogy, there must be no doubt as to Doris's birth date especially as she explained in her biography why she passed herself off as two years older. She was only 15 when she began her career as a singer in Barney Rapp's big band in 1939.

Now, something personal happened last year. As almost 30 years ago, I ordered a personal astrological chart but only for three months.

Following, the first day's personal prediction:

Aug 22 2016

Jupi quincunx Uran

Serious electrical problems can occur in the home requiring serious re-wiring, or electronic gear can burn out at this time, costing a great deal of money to be repaired.

Right the next day when I wanted to ride my bicycle, I found the heavy electrical problem on the e-bike kept in the house. I wrote the following e-mail August 23, 2016, at 3:17 p. m. to the Leon Cyle company:

Ladies and gentlemen,

Unfortunately, after only about 240 km I have a problem with my bicycle.

The battery is full, but the electric drive does not turn on.
The error display shows 09.

70

Please let me know what to do.

Best regards

Marianne E. Meyer

Only afterward did I read in the Astro chart about the necessary new cabling or electronic equipment and informed Mr. Hirsch about it. I suggested sending the parts so that hubby can repair it himself or Ezekiel, our competent car electrician. I didn't want to waste the best time to cycle. Sending the bike to Hannover and back takes at least three weeks. Unfortunately, everything went completely different. After 53 e-mails and as much scribbling as I could have invested in half a book, I had my bike back in mid-November! It has indeed cost a lot. For example, €118 at the post office. There it took three weeks to determine that they could not ship lithium batteries. The money I have as I said so far still not gotten back though they got mail from a lawyer friend of Joáo the guy Peter gave a Million for the Quinta do Vale golf project in Monte Francisco and a Julio Iglesias concert.

But the reason why it took so long, and for Leon Cycle and me it was so expensive, was again the lack of open-mindedness. I had sent the section of the astrological chart and asked to send me new cables. They only sent another sensor, which was not the problem. In this direction I always experience the same thing:

People mostly acknowledge themselves proudly as realists and do not realize that with their blinders they only hurt themselves.

IIf you still have doubts about the stars, you can read biographies of celebrities with the same birthday or place as yours. It is fascinating to compare their characteristics and milestones of life with your own. I have worked out this with Marianne Sägebrecht in the book Family Code, but it was more related to numerology.

Telepathy or after-death contact?

Could it not be that many of what we assume as telepathy represent after-death contacts? I came across this idea through my brother's experience in Paris. He had visited the French metropolis for the first time with his handball pals. The men stopped here and there for a bite to eat or a drink. When they wanted to head back to the hotel, the driver announced his being lost. All of a sudden, my brother had a vision of an illustrated 3-D map of Paris, so he could easily orient himself in the city of love. He directed the astonished sports mates on a different, particularly picturesque route, back to the hotel. I thought about Henry Miller as the channel, who knew all about Paris as you can read in his book *Quiet Days in Clichy.* He may have been another relative wanting to bail out his grand-nephew or great-grandnephew and namesake. For my father's grandfather had emigrated to the USA in 1902 and was said to have lived in the Carmel area. Henry's father was a tailor from Bavaria, and his mother grew up in Hesse. Our hometown Michel-stadt is on Shanks's pony distance from the tri-border area Baden-Wuerttemberg, Bavaria, and Hesse. The literary ambitions of my father, brother, grandmother Maryland my own might speak for it. Henry Miller also lived near Carmel for ten years.

As I explained in my water books, I assume that channeling at soul level happens through the water. In addition to Samuel Hahne-mann, who has documented that water stores information about 200 years ago, there are many modern researchers who no longer doubt this property of $H2O$. In the case of the high-potentials, with umpteen times of shaking of homeopathic remedies, no single mol-ecule of the original active substance is contained in the water.

Nevertheless, the frequencies of these means are effective. Our body water was also a river, cloud, and food water which has stored information over time. By the way, this also applies to cosmic water. We could know this for twenty years since in 1997, NASA published a photo showing enormous snowballs falling from space. Every day, a few thousand are coming to us, but they will disintegrate and become part of a cloud as soon as they are near the earth, according to NASA press release of May 1997. Like comet-like heavenly bodies of about 12 meters in diameter, snowballs have fallen billions of years from space indicating a continuous flow of cosmic information.

https://apod.nasa.gov/apod/ap970530.html

And have you not once before noticed that you are more likely to dream of your loved ones in the hereafter in rain or atmospheric humidity? Is our body water resonating with the cosmic water?

What is it with the number 11?

The number 11 is a recurrent issue to me, mainly as a date of death. My loved ones and friends have an 11 in their date of death. Could this be a message? The 11 is supposed to be a symbol of the connection between heaven and earth.

Or did I provoke the whole thing myself with my behavior? For, Peter's mother left her body on 11.11. 1987 at 11:11 a.m. Pacific Time. She was in a hospital in Wilhelmshaven and came to haunt me in our bedroom in Hermosa Beach. I told everybody about this phenomenon. I often said: "This was a clever move of Lisa to choose this date of death. Their sons will always remember the start of the carnival. Almost all those who knew about it made their transition on the 11th day, the 11th month, the year 11, or the cross total 11. My father on 1.10.1998 = digit sum 11. For my friend Ingrid who had known my parents, it was probably more important, to die between the birthday of my father and my mother, on June 5, 2009. But if you take the day and month, and the year extra, she'd also made a double 11. My girlfriend Marita had a fatal accident on 11.9.2001, spectacularly one hour before the collapse of the WTC towers. Jocelyn Brando even changed her plane of existence and vibration frequency on my birthday, on 27.11.2005. On this day many friends called. In bright sunshine with Californian temperatures, I was amazed that I cried at almost every call. On the following Easter, I painted Jocelyn a card with her favorite daffodil flowers. I had a hunch and tried to call her first. After I had not reached her, I checked the Internet and said: "Oh, wow, on my birthday. How did you do that?" My mother left her sick body on 1-1-11, Peter on 2-11-17.

Longing for reunion

Three and a half months, but it still hurts. The grief comes in waves but ebbs away more quickly. Perhaps it has to do with the book that I suffer more. I am always in the psychological dilemma, whether I better not write about Peter and me, but I couldn't help doing it. I consider it my task, for Peter, for me, Peter's relatives and friends, and for my readers who also may go through this process of grieving.

I realize that through the regularity of my daily routine I succeed in experiencing moments of positive feelings despite all the pain. When I walk the dogs through the wild nature in the morning and evening, collecting wood, flowers or soil, I find comfort in these regular activities.

5-24: The challenges are growing. Now the washing machine is broken. Maybe something blocks the drain again. We had this twice, last time it was big coins. But the repair was always a lot of work. The marble slab has to be lifted off, and the washing machine to be hauled outside. What Peter was doing, I do not know exactly. I think he let the water run through the garden hose and somehow managed to solve the blockade. I thought I could do something more easily with a flexible wire or the like right at the site. But so far I have found nothing suitable. So I will do the usual task on Friday. Perhaps Peter will inspire me.

Tomorrow, our choir sings mostly Portuguese songs, including Canção do Mar, in an old residential complex with a connected kindergarten in Santa Catarina.

https://www.youtube.com/watch?v=pgqCBgpZTsQ

Too bad, tomorrow Helga will also come. She is in a hurry and wants to be in Germany in ten days. I hope we can see each other again. But I can not stay away because the choir would miss my soprano voice. I told Helga not to be afraid of anything at the moment. She said, "that's coming again, it was the same with me. I had booked a helicopter flight in the USA. Everyone else had shit on their pants. But now I'd not do it anymore. Now I'm back to life." However, I think she might not have the insight that Peter gave me. Helga may be less sure what to expect. I know from experience as a young woman, and now from Peter and the many books, I have read about the after-death experiences. Life in the hereafter is, in any case, better than life on earth.

I'm still in the phase where I would rather be with Peter than to muddling along here. What Bolko on February 22 has shown Isabel, me on the book fair, sitting at the table and signing my successful book is not tempting me. It arouses not a bit anticipation in me. Worldly success and possession do not comfort me. For Peter, I would have liked to be rich. But now I'm not interested anymore. And since I've seen the other world, worldly pleasures are less desirable than ever. I will write the book about the car dealership as long as Peter is committed to helping me. Although I have already covered some of it in Family Code. Since Peter did not read any of my twenty books, he probably did not know that yet.

After-death contacts with musicians, old masters, and famous surgeons

Psychic surgeons, musicians, painters and other interactive souls may seem absurd to many. But let us only think of the genius kids. The modern Mozart, Jay Greenberg, demanded a cello as a toddler. In a music shop, he got a miniature cello. Jay took the bow and immediately began to play emotionally and with force. Up to the age of 12, he composed five symphonies, the Storm in a few hours. He speaks of multiple channels, and the music comes involuntarily, just filling his head.

http://www.wimp.com/musicprodigy

The psychic painter shown on the following video is another example of channeling from the other side:

www.youtube.com/watch?v=URM8KGpjztE

Shirley MacLaine watched Luiz Antonio Gasparetto in his home in Orange, California. Henri de Toulouse Lautrec came through and talked about her former life as a prostitute in Paris. No wonder Irma la Douce brought her an Oscar nomination. My girlfriend Dr. Ingrid Dennerlein-Barnack had previously translated for Antonio in Brazil. Luiz paints in trance old masters with crayons and color tubes. The deceased masters use him as a channel to tell us: Look, we still exist!

In the following video of 1981, we can see how Antonio channels a message from the master during the painting of a Toulouse Lautrec picture. The latter is glad that he is still connected to the physical world and thru Antonio has a way of working world-changing. At minute 3:27, he says that electronic devices might replace the mediumism or contact with the hereafter. He was right. I have just experienced this with Peter. It is also eminent that we are open to interactions with our loved ones on the other side because otherwise we'll not perceive their contact at all or dismiss it as a coincidence and forget it at once. Of course, they then give up.

https://www.youtube.com/watch?v=bWpc71VKiDI

Also, the souls of Dr. Barnard, Dr. Sauerbruch, and other famous surgeons work via spiritual healers such as Oprah Winfrey in the following videos:

https://www.youtube.com/watch?v=smjWQninbUY

https://www.youtube.com/watch?v=MenNIoHiO5Y

The spiritual world is still working with us on many other projects. It would be a blessing for all of us if science could cease to be blind to the fact that after we have left our bodies, we will continue to exist in the immaterial world! As long as scientists still wear their blinders, we can research ourselves and find out what the spiritual world wants to tell us. For what we learn from experience is real science. When we realize that love is the only power, the only God, we need not fear anything and least of all death. If we know who we are, we are free.

Near-death experiences and their aftermath

The fact that it is easier to live without the burden of the afflicted body has already been experienced by many. I too had an out-of-body experience as a consequence of an accident. While resting in bed, I suddenly found myself on a different level of existence in a circle of utterly familiar beings. I knew all about them and was aware of everything. The intense feeling of unity, the infinite ocean of unconditional love, I felt far more pleasant than anything I had ever experienced. That's why I felt sadness and emptiness when I was back in the body. I doubted I could experience anything like this in the physical world. Certain kinds of music may be enchanting too, but no comparison. Since that time, I have often been homesick for the heavenly realms.

Notably fascinating is the near-death experience of the neurosurgeon Eben Alexander, who was in a coma with bacterial meningitis for one week. His entire neocortex, that is, the brain part responsible for consciousness, no longer functioned. His chance of survival was 3%. During this time, Alexander had been confronted with a reality he had considered impossible. He had dived into a world of pure, bright, white-golden light. It was the "most peculiar, most beautiful world" he had ever seen. Alexander reviewed his journey into the hereafter according to strict scientific criteria and realized that we are all part of a universal, immortal consciousness. He realized that the death of the body and the brain is not the end of consciousness. For him, it is crystal clear that there is indeed life after death! (2016)

The oncologist Dr. Jeffrey Long reviewed brain physiological or chemical explanations of the near-death phenomenon. He is convinced of its reality. His captivating and poignant case histories of people of all ages and cultures give us an insight into the hereafter and confirm that the journey continues (2010).

5-26: I'm feeling fatigued. The worst was the large marble slab. Then the towing of the washing machine.

Outside I filled several times water into the hose, and after a few dark rags were washed out, I made a test run. The pumping and spinning were okay again.

5-27: Renate was there with the children. She asked if she could help me put the marble slab back on. I said, "No, never mind. Let's wait until Jochen is back. I prefer to wash once again. Somehow I feel that this is not over yet. Murphey's Law has hit all over the past few weeks, the two broken wrist watches I have not even mentioned."

It is nice that Renate comes once in a while. I am not a person going out often. Therefore I like it when people come to me.

I watch the 24-hour race. Maybe Peter is with me. After all, he'd raced through the Green Hell several times. I think of the race when the old "Striezel" Stuck took 3rd place with his team at the beginning of the 21st century and had his "most difficult 24-hour race of all times". Then hubby, nine years Stuck's senior raced the North Loop five hours during the night. Peter's young racing fellows had driven less quickly in the dark, so he took part of their time with his Spirulina tuned gimlet eyes.

Now I have to drag the washing machine out again and unscrew the cover because I had not fastened a screw nut and a part struck on the drum on the spin. But I am so knocked out from lifting the 160 x 70 cm marble slab that I will transport the washer tomorrow. 5-28: Rineke invited me. She is worried because I've lost weight. She thinks I don't care for me properly. I said I take three full meals, but I walk a lot more with the dogs. She said I'd muffle lately, whether I do not wash. Shock, but it is courageous of her, I thought. I bathe as always every morning, use the Lacoste pen - of little use I guess - I better take Peters spray from now on. On Tuesdays, I make errands before singing. It can be with a weak Deo, and because I smell nothing. From now on, I have to change undershirt, T-shirt or blouse every day. All have to be washed fresh at least as long until my sense of smell is back. So I quickly have to seal the discharge pump of the washing machine. Their flexible tube now has a hole. In any case, I am grateful to Rineke; I should have guessed it because I smell nothing. I have noticed the typical cuddly blanket smell already in others but had not the courage to say something. However, in such an extreme situation I could probably do it.

I've just given me a vitamin B-12 injection into the bottom muscle noticing the pain sensation also almost gone. Before B-12 shots were quite painful, much more than other agents, even for a while after the injection, but I do not feel any pain.

5-31: Three and a half months have passed. The grief work was very hard, but nowadays I'm beginning to see a silver lining is on the horizon. Nicole has just sent me a text message because I thanked her for her letter. She has her birthday on the same day as I, and we both have problems with the status quo. Nicole suggested borrowing a VW bus in Argentina and travel through South America. Peter and I wanted to do it with the camper. I had also encouraged him. Many Germans are in South America with their campers and sometimes leave them there and fly home in the summer. But Peter did not have the right drive. That is why I am convinced that in spirit he would accompany us.

6-14: Yesterday I picked up the TV before the choir rehearsal. I told the young man that I would like to test it so as not to have to come back if it did not work. He said, "this is not possible, you have to do it at home." I had forgotten the remote control again. At home, I opened the cardboard box, and there was a whole new one. Only then did I realize that it is a smaller one.

Today I went with Sigrid again to Conforama and said: "I brought my lawyer friend to be on the safe side." And then, Sesame opened, and the company gave me a more expensive brand name TV since there were only small Nevirs left, but I did claim to have a 40-inch television. Hopefully bye bye Murphy!

6-16: Usually, I do not bake cakes in the morning. But yesterday evening I forgot the chia seeds I use as an egg substitute. I had to mix the dough with the soaked seeds again. Linseeds go as well. I filled the dough into the baking tray, switched on the gas, and started baking. After doing some housework, I turned on my laptop. Until it was booted, I did the dishes. Suddenly, the light above the stove went on and off several times as if to signal SOS. I said, oh, the laptop, but at the same moment, I thought of the cake, and it was high time, just before burning. THANKS, Peter! I hope my sense of smell will return soon. I used to cook according to the law: As soon as the scent strokes my nose it's done.

In memory of Claus-Peter Christian Adolf Meyer

On February 11, 2017, at 15:15 Claus-Peter, the great love of my life was snatched from life, felled like a tree just as he always wanted to die. His oldest son Jens-Peter with Bianca, the younger son Arnd with Michaela, their children Katja, Anika and Marika as well as his brother Joachim with Renate, Anna and her family as well as many friends and relatives, mourn with me, his widow Marianne Erika.

Claus-Peter was born on February 4, 1942, as the oldest of two brothers of the married couple Lisa and Ernst-Peter in Wilhelmshaven. The war years the family spent in Gut Moorbeck. Early on, little Peter learned how to pursue his inclination, the car driving. He could barely look over the steering wheel but explored Wilhelmshaven's neighborhood with his brother Jochen. At school, CP was allowed to turn an honorary round. And because his teacher tormented him not only with neck-banging, he got to visit the boarding school on the island of Wangerooge. Is it by chance that the substitute daughter Mandira has just inherited the house of the health practitioner Rosi on Wangerooge, who years ago vainly pecked Peter with needles to quit smoking? But he handled it all alone through his will some ten years ago.

After a mechanic's apprenticeship at Opel, Claus-Peter married the 17-year-old Erika Harms at the tender age of 19 as a sturdy lineage holder was underway. During this time, he sold trucks for Daimler Benz until his father offered to finance business studies and support the family. Ernst-Peter imagined that his elder could work in his wine, tobacco, and spirits trade company, conducted with partner Klett. But nothing came of it because Ernst-Peter died shortly after Claus-Peters studies. Three and a half years after Jens-Peter a new earth citizen saw the light of the world. In the absence of a name, since the married couple had reckoned firmly with a girl Arnd was named via name book. Claus-Peter started his career as a managing assistant at Karstadt. So, he slowly worked his way towards the south, from where he could practice his motorsport easier. During his work as a computer organizer in the Metallgesellschaft in Frankfurt, Peter was able to take off from work to get his racing cars in the Academic Motorsport team Akamot. His favorite car was the red Glas. When he looked at it together with Erika, the latter said, "I saw it in his eyes, he would have bought it even if it hadn't had any wheels." Peter told me this just in the last days. I think he knew about his final farewell as did my father who passed on 10-1-98. He wrote on his last yearly ring binder "until the end of Sept. 98". Peter had disposed of almost all his documents.

The couple divorced after ten years of marriage. The sons remained with the mother, who married Peter's former rally co-driver Lothar Redelfs. After a two-year relationship with Ute Schaupensteiner, Peter lived with his Wilhelmshaven friend Eckhard Drexler in Frankfurt for six months. There, after a half-year intermezzo as a manager assistance at a fur trader, he started a second-hand car dealership because his tax consultant advised him that he would be better off with trading something because of his income from renting and leasing. One of his first cars Peter dealt was a light blue cost-cutting beetle, which I, the social pedagogy student Marianne Holschuh, discovered in the Frankfurter Rundschau in February 1974. Immediately I drove to my future husband Claus-Peter with the beetle of my friend Heinz-Peter, who was also born in WHV. We got married on November 4, 1980, on the day of Ronald Reagen's election.

It was in the penultimate year of our ten-year stay in California that Peter was seeking contact with his sons after some 40 years of lacking communication. I still see the glow in his eyes when he held the two-page fax from Jens-Peter in his hands. He was always proud of his sons and thankful that Lothar has taken such good care.

Back in Germany, Claus-Peter worked as a test driver for AMG Mercedes at the Nürburgring where Arnd was working as the guru for the chassis engineering. The life with Peter was neither mediocre nor dull or safe. Whenever it had once again turned to a high level of emotional pressure, Peter always said you'd have better married an accountant. A line of my astrological chart crosses my mind: The need for change is important. Peter had always taken care of that.

The one thing Peter regretted in his exciting life was that he had not done more to become a professional racing driver. The time when he was dealing with cars was his happiest years. In his last two races with his MGB in Las Vegas and Palm Springs in 1998, he finished first and second. Peter from the other side asked me on February 2017, mediated by Isabel Bannier-Groß, to write about the car dealer times in Frankfurt and Los Angeles some day. Five days before, he had shown me his bright, warm new world, and looked extremely happy. Peter lives in a much better world. I miss him so much and would like to be with him now on the other side.

Epilogue of the first (German) edition

Shall we let the dead rest? Some people I'm dealing with affirm this question. They include Inge Schneider, the director of the Jupiter publishing house, whom I would like to thank on this occasion for reviewing the manuscript and her comments.

I do not think I cling to the hereafter, even if it seems so in my present situation. Losing both parents, I'd never hold on to them. Nevertheless, they both report at certain times, but by themselves.

Only during the tests with the water crystal photos, I asked my father a question. In the sudden death of my husband, on the sixth post-mortal day, I followed the advice of my friend Carole Madrid: Placing my left hand on the heart and the right hand on the solar plexus I looked in the north direction and called Peter to come. All of a sudden I was with Peter in his surroundings. He took my hand and showed me around. The area reminded me of Morocco.

One day before the memorial ceremony, I called Peter again. I woke up at night by a sound, snapped the knife on the nightstand. It was not a burglar, but Peter. He was standing in front of my bed. I flew into his arms. He wore another garment of importance: the gray sweater knitted by me. I felt the soft material on my hands for a while. Peter had considerably rejuvenated since our last meeting. It seems to be a common phenomenon. I told my egg lady the experience. Fernanda said she had experienced this with her mother as well. She had appeared young and beautiful in Fernanda's bedroom and had laid into bed next to her for a while. It was a very comforting experience.

The sea burial with Sagres, Stones & Co. was the best funeral service ever experienced by all those present, and quite in the sense of Peter: pleasingly off-beat.

A summer month in Germany
I thought my stay in Germany with relatives and friends would be good for me. Maybe I wanted to test whether I could live in Germany again. I think so, but I guess I'd be homesick for the Algarve climate.

About 40 years ago we drove with our Dalmatian friend Bebóo in the Japanese Embassy Mercedes with a flag-bearer onto the island of Sylt. That was the only time I could breathe Hamburg air.

When I informed my Hamburg friend Barbara Simonsohn about the death of my husband, she consoled me with an offer: a visit to Hamburg and one of two seminar freebies: either a deacidification seminar or a Reiki-1 initiation. Since I have long had the first three Reiki grades, I thought of deacidifying. But after three tearful months, I already had ample deacidification since emotional tear contain poisons. In California, where I got Reiki, I was able to notice tremendous changes, especially in the first degree. That's why I decided for the four initiations of the 1st Reiki grade held in a beautiful old building with stucco ceilings. When I gave a full treatment for a woman teaching at the university, it was similar as many years ago with my friend Hilde who I met at a New Year's Eve party in Brentwood. She had a swollen cheek and severe pain. The dentist had said the swelling would have to subside before he could pull the tooth. As a dedicated Reiki novice, I offered Hilde to be my first guinea pig. She said, go ahead, it won't hurt.

As I held my right hand on Hilda's cheek, it was so tingling that I started to giggle and said I do not know if I could endure it for a long time. Three days later Hilde called. I asked, what about your tooth? She said the pain and the swelling were gone the next day and the dentist said, I can keep the tooth.

Treating the docent, I felt a tingling in my right hand during the second and third positions. Both hands became extremely hot. After we had finished, Christina said: "Strange, for some time I had a pain here pointing to the right groin. It's all gone."

All the participants glowed with nourished souls and centered forces. Reiki, the universal life energy harmonizes and balances body, mind, and soul. This way we collect ourselves, to gather our thoughts finding peace in the restlessness of daily life.

Barbara showed me in the following days, where she jogs along the Elbe every morning. I was also allowed to admire her vegetable and fruit garden. She made me acquainted with her 97-year-old, still agile father Wilhelm Simonsohn, known for his award-winning autobiography. The visit of a park on the Elb-Chaussee and the botanical garden rounded off my visit to Hamburg harmoniously. It is nice to be able to travel with a day ticket for € 6,20 not only with the railways but also on the ships in Hamburg to the most remote parts of the city. Maybe next time I will go to a concert in the Elbphilharmonie, so I can also enter the harmonious halls of the gigantic structure. But the view around the green city with the numerous bridges is already a pleasure. There was still a musical highlight. Barbara is the youngest member of the excellent senior choir of her church community. We have been practicing half an hour before, so I'd been able to sing along courageously. The conductor invited me to sing in the choir. I would if I'd live in Hamburg. A 90-year-old surprised me with his voice. He even delivered the notes. There must be something rejuvenating in the Hamburg air. I just think about Helmut Schmidt, whom I've seen in a photograph together with Barbara's even-aged father on the wall of his living room. I enjoyed the week with Barbara Simonsohn since we have a similar way of thinking, living, and eating.

The following two weeks with my girlfriend Ursula Keim and her daughter, on the other hand, required to get used to. But I'm pretty adaptable. Renée Stellwag, who lost her husband three years ago by pancreatic cancer had expensive ghost-buster instruments, and I spent two nights with her. It came out that Peter had apparently fallen victim to an accident. That was my first impression as well. Peter had worked with electricity in the rain. I will ask Isa once again to ask Peter before I ask about the results of the autopsy. My last week I spent at my brother's, in the modernized and reduced apartment of my mother. I was pleasantly surprised by my nephew's

87

lively family life and how warm and friendly Andreas handled his sons. Philipp, my youngest great-nephew, received me particularly charmingly. He is the most talented soccer player, who as a five-year-old already used to flank and now sometimes shoots five goals in a game. Three Bundesliga clubs in the area would like to train him. But the 12-year-old would rather stay at home instead of living in a boarding school suffering homesickness, longing for friends and family. But this should not be the end of Philip's future career. In any case, remaining in the family will be an advantage for his emotional development.

During the landing approach, the plane had shaken vigorously because of strong winds. I used to be afraid. Now I was quite relaxed, almost happy. The taxi from the airport to the train station of Faro, about 7 km, cost €10.50 but on the train, I had to pay only 1.50 for about 35 km. The train travel must be subsidized by the State or taxpayer respectively because regular train tickets are also much cheaper than in Germany. It is also less stressful to buy a ticket. No need to wasting time at the counter, or at a ticket machine. You sit comfortably on the train, and a train attendant takes the money.

Renate found me at Lidl, whose branch is right next to the station. Convenient for commuters, annoying for customers who are looking for a shaded parking lot. Renate just came from the gym and took me home as agreed by phone.

Life goes on

After the many people-to-people contacts in Germany, the loneliness in which I live became startlingly clear to me. The misery lasted a few days until I had brought home and garden back to mint.

I must bring the car to the auto-shop because it loses oil, and all the warning lights are on. Washer kaputt, car kaputt ...

Helga has just sent this link via WhatsApp: https://www.airbnb.de/s/Faro--Faro--PT/homes? selected_listing_id

Yes, living is inexpensive here. If I were to live in Germany, my savings would be spent in about ten years and I would have to ap- ply for a state pension increase. Here I do not need to eat up my savings. Perhaps I can still lure some German retirees, relatives, and friends to settle here because here they can afford much more with their pension. Portugal leads following Iceland and New Zealand the Global Peace Index as the most peaceful country. It is true that I have to compromise if I only think of the odd behavior of the post office and the power station denying me my money. But overall, I can live here much better than in the cold homeland. Nevertheless, I would like to live in summer in Germany, in win- ter in the Algarve. When we were still living in the Marktstraße in Frankfurt-Bergen, I often passed the town writer's house thinking of living there for a year, if I were alone. At that time I lived with Peter in a much more luxurious house with a pool and wanted to be a writer living in a small farm hose.

8-2: Fortunately only the fuel hose was leaky. There was no oil, but gasoline leaking. Perhaps a beast had nibbled away the hose when I was gone.

I have not cried all day long, and I am reading the Isabel Allende's "The House of Spirits" for the fourth time because I have no more unread book. And then there is a passage in the book, and the water trickle down the cheeks again. Two children from different social backgrounds love each other. They enjoy the daybreak in the mud. Expressing her feeling of happiness the girl said, "when I'm grown up, we marry and live on the Three Marias." The boy shook his head as he already knew his place in the world. Pedro also knew that he would always love Blanca and this daybreak would continue in his memory. This picture would accompany him dying. I would probably have cried as well since it is not unusual for me to be overwhelmed by feelings.

8-12: Since I stripped my bed today, the "The House of Spirits" has disappeared. It seemed to have been swallowed up by the earth. Neither behind nor under the bed I found it. I remember my Californian friend once reported such an incident. Leanne missed a gemstone or an earring that had disappeared from a place in the bathroom. Several weeks later, at this very place, it reappeared. But this long I didn't want to wait and took a book from Dexter Dias from the shelf, which I liked as well: Rule of Law. The first war crimes prosecution since Nuremberg.

I searched a few more times in all rooms, but the Ghost House remained missing.

8-18: Last night I talked to Peter because I had planned to bring the car to the mechanics so that they could fix it to get the MOT certificate. I thought if the car needs extensive repair I'd rather buy another one. Since about the last 2000 km it's got a noise probably from the hydraulic. Besides, Peter said, the joint shaft may soon have to be exchanged.

I started around 8.30 a. m. In front of the garage, just as I tried to get into the first gear to get uphill the gear change was no more working. A sign? I'll see how much it costs and then must decide. Since the guys open at 9:00 a. m., I cleaned the car a bit. When they arrived and opened the workshop, there was the car I would like to have next, a GPL Polo.

8-21: In a dream, I was with my mother at an open-air quiz. I could barely breathe. In the last dream sequence, I indicated that I would like to go on a backpacking trip. As I woke up at 5:15 a.m., I had actual problems breathing and let off some air. Apparently the beer. Our racing Englishwoman Shirl had once again approached one of our dogs, but Tobi escaped with no more than a fright. But the terror was tremendous. Never before had I seen such an angry and nervous dog. I took Tobi into the house and spoke calmly to him. Then I remembered that I still have a few bottles of beer. I opened one, filled him a small bowl, and put the rest in the refrigerator. The rest I had drunk the evening before. I will no more do this and rather ask the Google boys and girls what else can be done with beer.

http://www.menshealth.com/guy-wisdom/new-uses-for-beer

After drinking a glass of water with soda, I wanted to read to get tired and to sleep another hour. I grabbed next to me for what I thought the Dexter Dias ... but the words of the opened book were all in German. I closed it and saw red. There was no more thinking about sleep. "Well, Peter, where did you hide the Ghost House all the time?" And just like with Leanne, it reappeared in the same place I had it last.

8-26: Speaking of reading, end of February, I lent Sigrid the book "The Wheel of Life: A Memoir of Living and Dying" by Elisabeth Kübler-Ross. Since my friend doesn't believe in a life after life, I wanted to convince her. I had chosen the biography because I thought it would be more entertaining than the other books of the scientist. About three months ago, I asked if I could have the book back. I had marked a few things and wanted to see if I could quote anything. Sigrid obstinately persisted in saying that I had not lent her a book. Because of my near blindness as a child, I have a strong visual memory. I still visualize her standing with a pink sweater and black jeans next to me on the bookshelf. Today, in the café in front of the market hall, I sat together with Sigrid, her son and her sister-in-law, with whom I was talking about my books. When I gave her the flyer, she said the Family Code I've seen at a friend's. That amazed me since the book is not exactly a hit. Somehow we got back to the borrowed book. When Sigrid went back to the market hall, I said, "I've had something like this with my aunt. I asked Anneliese for a green tea. But she brought a fruit tea. I said I don't agree with fruit tea. It is too acidifying. I only drink green tea. She said this is green tea. I held out the red bag, but that did not help. She hangs on stubbornly and stiffly that it was green tea. I would be interested in how much percent of all seniors will develop such senile stubbornness. By the way, I made a serious mistake in the lending matter. I had seen "The Wheel of Life" in the free books box at Petra's health food store. I should have taken a closer look at it. It may have been my very copy. Since I had received it from my mother, it would be nice if it would reappear. With all the coincidences in my life, my book may be falling into my hands again at a flea market. But basically, nothing important anymore. If one loses the only confidant - a piece of self - can get over all other losses easily. I have to live my life to the end and be careful not to lose myself in memories.

9-13: I just got an e-mail from Rolf Keppler, the descendant of the famous Johannes, mathematician, astronomer, and astrologer. It included interesting reports. Mr. Jebens experience report about his drive with Nikola Tesla in his aether energy powered Pierce Arrow (tinyurl.com/yd2o85nk and tinyurl.com/ybvn9uvo) I immediately devoured and forgot the cake again. "Thank you, Peter, Fortunately, you saved this one from burning also by suddenly flashing the oven light. And I wondered today you must be somewhere else since I didn't notice you for some days. Still longing for you ...".

9-29: Sometimes I still blame myself. In the morning, passing by Peter's picture, I said: "Was it up to me that you were not feeling well anymore? Often when you had your evening wine, you said you would like to be dead. Should I have pampered you more or did you feel not enough loved or anything? In the late afternoon, I walked the dogs head down to look for some beautiful stones for my rock garden. Within less than two minutes I found five stone hearts. For days before, I was always looking for them not finding any. Thank you, Peter! So I was not the reason that you often said after your usual wine quantity, "I would like to be dead."

10-5: I didn't turn on the washing machine outside until late afternoon. When it was getting dark, I closed the front door. When the washer pumped off at around 5:00 pm, I did not hear that, because I was focused revising Dr. C's book. This editorial work I owe Barbara Simonsohn. Already 20 years ago she had recommended my thesis on spirulina and the immune system to the Windpferd Publishing house who then released my all-time bestseller *Spirulina, das blaugrüne Wunder* selling 80,000 copies.

Suddenly I felt my mother around me. I said, oh, Mom, that's a rare visit. What are you doing here, is something wrong? At the same moment, I remembered the washing machine and went outside. The hose had slipped, the water was gone. I clamped the hose between the water pipe and the cistern wall, let in the new water and returned to the laptop. "Thanks, Mom, that was high time. Could you remember if I'll forget the last pumping again?" While working for some time, I heard a knocking sound from the next room. "Oops! Is it time again?" Indeed, the wash cycle had stopped and I collected the water in buckets. When I pulled the laundry out after spin-drying and cumbersome stuffed it into a huge bag, I thought of Mother's saying "just like in ancient Rome" and said, "yes, Mom, that's how it is at the moment. There will come better times again. But this semi-automatic washing machine is better than the huge copper kettle in the laundry room where you used to do the laundry 60 years ago. It's also hard for me to part from the washer because you gave it to me. "

All at once it occurred to me that Ma was also there because I had forgotten Grandma Maria's birthday. Immediately I got a white candle and lit it.

10-18: After revising Barbara's Artemisia book, "Your Third Brain" by Dr. Marco Ruggiero, MD followed. The boss of the Jim Humble publishing house, Leo Koehof, seemed to be satisfied with my work otherwise, he would not have forced the partly miserably translated book by Dr. Leonhard Coldwell on me. I'm struggling for three weeks already. Anyone who has read my FAMILY CODE book knows that I said to my friend Celeste, who was reading screenplays for MGM for eight years: I would also like to earn money by reading books. Although it is now something more than just reading, but also fun. Is that what Peter mentally taught me on Feb. 11, a few minutes after my goodbye kiss in the morgue of the hospital? Everything is fine, even for you, you will soon realize that. Had he everything already seen, waiting for me?

10-20: The last three nights I dreamed of Peter. Maybe that's a sign that he's more with me again. The eye drops helping keep the pressure down on the left eye doesn't help at the right one. But I do not want to go to the doctors again. The one in Faro was a typical aloof not at all eloquent contemporary. The second one in Tavira was a little more talkative, but except prescribing a remedy three times as expensive and measuring the pressure, NADA! The suspicion immediately crept into my gray cells, there was probably once again a representative of the pharmaceutical industry with any bait turning up at the ophthalmologist's doorstep in case he prescribes this remedy to his patients. After three weeks, I stopped because the pain did not go away. I took the matter into my own hands.

Fortunately, the pharmacist is married to a yoga teacher, and it was not strange to him when I arrived with a pendulum hoping that my late husband may make a better choice. In the left eye, I drip Latanoprost and into the right Ganfort. That I could have a blue and a brown eye over time, I would not mind, has my bitch, too, but since Ganfort does not work, I'd like to try another remedy. He gave me Xalacom. I held the ring - a birthday present from Peter for my 50th - using as a pendulum over my left hand and asked, is this my left hand? The yes sign back and forth was a bit hesitant. But when I put the Xalacom box in my left hand asking is this a good remedy for my right eye?, the pendulum hit so hard that I thanked Peter with loud laughter. The Xalacom contains Latanoprost and as an additional active ingredient Timolol. I think it will help since for the last two weeks I am taking it, I'm thankful for not feeling pain.

11-9: Since Uli will fly back to Germany on November, 20 I've decided to bring my birthday feast forward. Anyway, I have set up this traditional dinner more for Peter's late mother Lisa who left her body on 11-11-1987. This way Peter's family was always together and I imagined that Lisa was with us. And from now on Peter will also be with us.

Literatur

Alexander, Eben: Proof of Heaven: A Neurosurgeon's Journey into the Afterlife. Simon & Schuster 2012,

Elmquist, Anders Leopold, My friend on the other side - the book about Friedrich Jürgenson who discovered voice phenomena from a fourth life dimension.: The scientific proof about the voices "from space". Kindle Edition 2016

Guggenheim, Bill and Judy: Hello from Heaven: A New Field of Research-After-Death Communication Confirms That Life and Love Are Eternal. Bantam 1997

Jürgenson, Friedrich: Sprechfunk mit Verstorbenen. München 1996

Kagan, Annie: The Afterlife of Billy Fingers: How My Bad-Boy Brother Proved to Me There's Life After Death, 2013 Newburyport, Mass 2013

Kübler-Ross, Elisabeth: On Life after Death. Celestial Arts, 2004

Long, Jeffrey: Evidence of the Afterlife: The Science of Near-Death Experiences . HarperOne 2011

Meyer, Marianne E.: Familien Code. Norderstedt 2016
How Water Connects our Worlds. Water Crystal Photos as a Mirror of the Soul, Norderstedt 2016
Spirulina, Survival Food for a New Era: Amazing Healing Success with the Blue-green Algae - Delicious Recipes with the Primal Nourishment. Norderstedt 16

Stead, Estelle: The Blue Island: and Other Spiritualist Writings (Life on Other Worlds Series). Square Circles Publishing 2013

Here you can share your near-death experiences with others and read them from others:

http://www.nderf.org

In this enchanting spiritual novel, you take part in Marianne's exciting life on four continents realizing that we are all interconnected, and families have their value system for generations.

This code of own rules, sayings and communication styles is also working when the family members live on different continents without knowing each other.

This autobiographical novel should be present in every household. (IBG).

The book represents a bridge connecting the land of the living and the beyond. It shows there is neither guilt nor chance or luck but cause and effect that can be poles apart for many centuries and incarnations. Happiness, sorrow, and coincidence are only concepts of the not perceived law. And if we don't want to learn we will suffer. The only thing remaining to connect the worlds, the meaning of life is LOVE.

978-3741282331 188 pages 17 x 22 cm €12,90

This exciting book wins by a clear statement on the mystery of change and storage ability of the water. Inge Schneider, head of the Swiss Jupiter-Verlag found in her book review in the NET-Journal the author's findings that the water is the "interface between the physical and metaphysical reality" particularly appealing.

The reader will find disturbing facts about the quality of commercial waters. Anyone who believes that a tap water is clean, is encouraged to think and act.

M. Meyer advises on activating water adequately. After all, who tastes for the first´time naturally vitalized, oxygenated and alkaline water from the tap, want to drink no more soda water from plastic bottles. Pure water is the ideal solution for all health problems, especially affecting the brain.

Ultimately, the author introduces free energy´researchers and their technologies. She also shows what to do, so space energy can soon flow in all households.

ISBN 978-3-7347-3691-9 104 p. 17x22cm €7,99

Through a friend in Topanga, the hippie community west of Los Angeles, the author came into contact with Uschi Obermaier, the mother of all supermodels. The female icon of the 68s already toured in the mid-70s in a luxury RV India, USA, and Mexico.

When in a picture story Marianne Meyer saw the sex symbol and her partner Dieter Bockhorn in their camping bus, the wish for such a house on wheels was born. This book in novel form is not a guidebook in the traditional sense. It depicts the lives of the caravans, who are overwhelmed in Morocco and have contact with the locals. Some readers regard the work as an occult experience report. We were all born with set talents. The author is to make people hope and motivate a healthy and fulfilling life. She also shows that there are more things between heaven and earth ... and how we can achieve what we want from life. Marianne Meyer's funny writing style. Readers write that they felt as if they had been there.

ISBN 978-3-7386-8482-7   94 p. 17x22cm €7,90

Marianne E. Meyer

Spirulina

Survival Food
for a New Era

Delicious Recipes with the Primal Nourishment

Amazing Healing Effects with the Blue-green Alga

Who needs Spirulina? We all do! Why? Because of infertile soils, we can hardly get any energy from our food. The blue-green microalga is concentrated solar power because it contains all the colors of the spectrum and thus all frequencies of light, just like the water of Lourdes.

More and more people supplement their diets with the beneficial protein food. And more and more dentists use it for discharging amalgam and other toxins.

Around the globe, sensational studies and reports prove: With Spirulina we can strengthen our immune system as well as stand up to pain, depression, diabetes, MS, cataracts, allergies, anemia, arthritis, liver fibrosis, Parkinson's disease, and even AIDS, cancer, and radium rays. Muchly benefiting from Spirulina are the sick, convalescent, heavy workers, athletes, stressed mothers, hyperactive children, the elderly, busy managers and our pets.

In this lovingly illustrated book with delicious recipes, each chapter is covered in note form; essential parts are highlighted. Coss-readers can attain a compact knowledge of the #1 superfood (AARP) in 30 minutes.

ISBN 978-3-7431-8541-8   104 p. 17x22 € 7,99